English Dictionary
for Young Learners

# My Words
# 564

with Japanese-English/
English-Japanese
Dictionary

# CONTENTS

**My Words 564** は、日本の子供達が自分で辞書をつくりながら語彙を学ぶ楽しさを体感できることを考えて創り出した「読んで」「書いて」「引く」辞書です。

本書は英語を学ぶ子供達に基本的な語彙を定着させることを目的につくられた前半と、子供達が自分の言いたいことを自分で調べ、その英語表現を使うことができる「発信型英語教育」のための辞書の2つのパートに分かれています。

前半の部分は英語を学ぶ子供達に確実に習得してほしい基本語彙564語を選び、33種類のカテゴリーに分けています。児童英語教育の範囲で習得が必須の語彙を示すことによって、ただ楽しいだけの英語教育に終わらせないようにしました。また、子供達も自分の習熟度をその都度知ることができるため、次第に語彙力に自信を持つことができるでしょう。

## My Words 564 (pp.1-47)の使い方は・・・

基本語彙564語に加え、動詞の過去形96語、名詞の複数形（不規則変化）等668語を練習します。カテゴリーごとに日本語に該当する英語の語彙を、クラスで「読み」、次に四線のグレー部分をなぞってスペルを「書き」ます。1ページごとに、**Flip-Flops**（使い方は下記参照）で英語の部分を隠して「日本語訳を見ながら英語を言う練習」、次に日本語の部分を隠して、「英語を見て発音し、日本語訳を言う練習」をしてください。なお、語彙の音声はQRで練習することができます。全668語を収録してありますので、リズムに合わせて何度も復唱してください。覚えた単語は、単語の左横の番号をぬって、覚えた語彙が増えていくことを目で確認していきましょう。簡単な和英辞書としても使えるようにしてあります。特に、◉の表示のある日本語には、「和英辞書」に例文を掲げてあります。

## 後半の「辞書」部分は・・・

「知りたい単語を自分で調べる」第一歩として使える「和英辞書」と「英和辞書」を用意しました。「和英辞書」には、そのまま使える平易な例文を紙面の許す限り掲載しました。自己表現を口語でおこなう時、あるいはクリエイティブ・ライティングの練習時に有効に利用してください。

この本を通して、子供達が語彙学習の楽しみを見出し、自分の知りたい語彙を辞書で調べ、習得することによって知っていく楽しみを体感できることを望んでやみません。　　　　　中本幹子

**My Words 564** was created for Japanese children to enjoy the process of learning vocabulary words by building their own dictionary as they read, write and look up words. It consists of two sections: the work section where children learn the basic 564 words in 33 categories and the dictionary section children can use as reference when expressing themselves in English.

After they learn the words from each category, use the **Flip-Flops** to check and reinforce the words. (See bottom for more on **Flip-Flops**.)

＊The audio QR codes contain recordings of all 688 words (564 basic words, 96 past tense words and some irregular plural forms). so that children can practice saying the words over and over again.

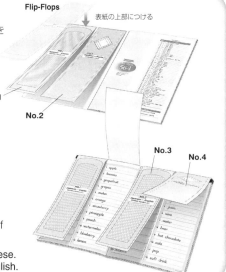

### 4つのFlip-Flopで単語チェック！

本書のカバーの折返し部分にあるNo.1〜4の**Flip-Flops**を切って、図のようにくっつけておき、単語を覚えたかどうか、調べたいページを隠してチェックしましょう。

◆**No.1, No.3**—英語を発音して日本語にしよう。
◆**No.2, No.4**—日本語を見て英語にしてみよう。

**Flip-Flops**はパタパタ動くこと、の意味から名づけました。

### Check how much you learned with Flip-Flops!

Cut out the **Flip-Flops** No.1-4 on the inside cover and tape them to the book as shown. Once a category is learned, use a **Flip-Flop** to hide one side of the page and try saying the translation of the covered words!

◆**No.1, No.3**—Read the English and say the Japanese.
◆**No.2, No.4**—Read the Japanese and say the English.

| # | | # | |
|---|---|---|---|
| 1 | | 1 | I |
| 2 | | 2 | you |
| 3 | | 3 | he |
| 4 | | 4 | she |
| 5 | | 5 | it |
| 6 | | 6 | they |
| 7 | | 7 | we |
| 8 | | 8 | my |
| 9 | | 9 | your |
| 10 | | 10 | his |
| 11 | | 11 | her |
| 12 | | 12 | me |

| | | 現在形 | 過去形 |
|---|---|---|---|
| 1 | （〜が）好き | like | liked |
| 2 | 住んでいる | live | lived |
| 3 | 知っている | know | knew |
| 4 | （〜を）持っている | have | had |
| 5 | （〜を）食べる | have | had |
| 6 | （家族や友達が）いる，（ペットを）飼う | have | had |
| 7 | （〜を）読む | read | read |
| 8 | （〜を）話す | speak | spoke |
| 9 | （〜を）書く | write | wrote |
| 10 | （〜が）ほしい | want | wanted |
| 11 | 〜したい | want to | wanted to |
| 12 | 勉強する | study | studied |

# Verbs／動詞 2

category
2

| | | 現在形 | 過去形 |
|---|---|---|---|

| 13 | 行く | 13 | go | went |
| 14 | 見る | 14 | look | looked |
| 15 | (〜を) 食べる | 15 | eat | ate |
| 16 | (〜を) 飲む | 16 | drink | drank |
| 17 | 言う | 17 | say | said |
| 18 | 歩く | 18 | walk | walked |
| 19 | ねむる | 19 | sleep | slept |
| 20 | 立つ | 20 | stand | stood |
| 21 | すわる | 21 | sit | sat |
| 22 | たずねる | 22 | ask | asked |
| 23 | 答える | 23 | answer | answered |
| 24 | (〜を) 愛している | 24 | love | loved |

| | 現在形 | 過去形 |
|---|---|---|
| 25 開ける | open | opened |
| 26 (〜を)与える, くれる | give | gave |
| 27 始まる | start | started |
| 28 終わる | finish | finished |
| 29 (〜を)教える | teach | taught |
| 30 (〜を)習う | learn | learned |
| 31 遊ぶ | play | played |
| 32 (チーム戦のスポーツを)する, (楽器を)ひく | play | played |
| 33 働く | work | worked |
| 34 (テレビを)見る | watch | watched |
| 35 来る | come | came |
| 36 (〜を)使う | use | used |

# Verbs／動詞 4

category 2

| | | 現在形 | 過去形 |
|---|---|---|---|
| 37 | 走る | run | ran |
| 38 | 歌う | sing | sang |
| 39 | 泳ぐ | swim | swam |
| 40 | スキーをする | ski | skied |
| 41 | スケートをする | skate | skated |
| 42 | 飛ぶ | fly | flew |
| 43 | おどる | dance | danced |
| 44 | 料理する | cook | cooked |
| 45 | 登る | climb | climbed |
| 46 | 切る | cut | cut |
| 47 | 運転する | drive | drove |
| 48 | 投げる | throw | threw |

five 5

| | 現在形 | 過去形 |
|---|---|---|

| 49 | 聞く | 49 listen | listened |
|---|---|---|---|
| 50 | しゃべる, 話す | 50 talk | talked |
| 51 | (〜を)えがく, かく | 51 draw | drew |
| 52 | (〜を)もらう, 受け取る | 52 get | got |
| 53 | (〜を)忘(わす)れる | 53 forget | forgot |
| 54 | (〜を)つかまえる | 54 catch | caught |
| 55 | (〜する)必要がある | 55 need | needed |
| 56 | (〜を)作る | 56 make | made |
| 57 | (〜を)手伝う | 57 help | helped |
| 58 | (〜を)話す, 伝える | 58 tell | told |
| 59 | (〜を)買う | 59 buy | bought |
| 60 | 止まる, やめる | 60 stop | stopped |

| | 現在形 | 過去形 |
|---|---|---|
| 61 聞こえる, (〜するのを) 聞く | hear | heard |
| 62 叫ぶ, 泣く | cry | cried |
| 63 (にっこり) 笑う, ほほえむ | smile | smiled |
| 64 思う, 考える | think | thought |
| 65 (〜に) 会う | meet | met |
| 66 のぞむ, 期待する | hope | hoped |
| 67 (〜を) 送る | send | sent |
| 68 (自転車などに) 乗る | ride | rode |
| 69 (〜を) 始める, 始まる | begin | began |
| 70 (〜を) 取る | take | took |
| 71 (〜を) 売る | sell | sold |
| 72 閉める | close | closed |

| | | 現在形 | 過去形 |
|---|---|---|---|

| 73 | （〜を）洗う | 73 wash | washed |
| 74 | そうじする, きれいにする | 74 clean | cleaned |
| 75 | （〜を）こわす, やぶる | 75 break | broke |
| 76 | （声を出して）笑う | 76 laugh | laughed |
| 77 | におう, においがする | 77 smell | smelled |
| 78 | （〜を）変える | 78 change | changed |
| 79 | 楽しむ | 79 enjoy | enjoyed |
| 80 | 去る, 出発する | 80 leave | left |
| 81 | （〜の）練習をする, けいこする | 81 practice | practiced |
| 82 | （〜を）理解する | 82 understand | understood |
| 83 | （〜を）支払う | 83 pay | paid |
| 84 | 見る, 会う | 84 see | saw |

| | | 現在形 | 過去形 |
|---|---|---|---|
| 85 | 着く | 85 reach | reached |
| 86 | 到着する | 86 arrive | arrived |
| 87 | 待つ | 87 wait | waited |
| 88 | 滞在する | 88 stay | stayed |
| 89 | （〜を）見つける | 89 find | found |
| 90 | （〜を）説明する | 90 explain | explained |
| 91 | （〜を）覚えている | 91 remember | remembered |
| 92 | 落ちる | 92 fall | fell |
| 93 | 押す | 93 push | pushed |
| 94 | 引く | 94 pull | pulled |
| 95 | えさを与える | 95 feed | fed |
| 96 | 叫ぶ | 96 shout | shouted |

# Verbal Phrases／動詞句 1

| | | | |
|---|---|---|---|
| **1** | 起きる | **1** | get up |
| **2** | 寝(ね)る | **2** | go to bed |
| **3** | 夜ふかしする | **3** | stay up late |
| **4** | 昼寝(ひるね)をする | **4** | take a nap |
| **5** | かたづける | **5** | put away |
| **6** | ふろに入る | **6** | take a bath |
| **7** | 散歩する | **7** | take a walk |
| **8** | 買い物に行く | **8** | go shopping |
| **9** | キャッチボールをする | **9** | play catch |
| **10** | ～に乗る | **10** | get on |
| **11** | ～から降(お)りる | **11** | get off |
| **12** | ～をさがす | **12** | look for |

| | | | |
|---|---|---|---|
| 13 | 列にならぶ | 13 | get in line |
| 14 | ～の世話をする | 14 | take care of |
| 15 | 旅行をする | 15 | go on a trip |
| 16 | 物音を立てる | 16 | make (a) noise |
| 17 | 楽しい時をすごす | 17 | have a good time |
| 18 | 逃げる | 18 | run away |
| 19 | ～出身である | 19 | be from |
| 20 | 静かにする | 20 | be quiet |
| 21 | (～に) 遅刻する | 21 | be late for |
| 22 | (～が) 得意である | 22 | be good at |
| 23 | (～が) 下手である | 23 | be poor at |
| 24 | (～を) 誇りに思う | 24 | be proud of |

| | | | |
|---|---|---|---|
| 1 | 1日 | 1 | one day |
| 2 | 1週間 | 2 | one week |
| 3 | 1か月 | 3 | one month |
| 4 | 1年 | 4 | one year |
| 5 | 時間 | 5 | hour |
| 6 | 分 | 6 | minute |
| 7 | 朝 | 7 | morning |
| 8 | 昼 | 8 | afternoon |
| 9 | 夕方 | 9 | evening |
| 10 | 今日 | 10 | today |
| 11 | 明日 | 11 | tomorrow |
| 12 | 昨日 | 12 | yesterday |

# Days of the Week & Seasons／曜日・季節

category
5

| | 日本語 | | 英語 |
|---|---|---|---|
| 1 | 日曜日 | 1 | Sunday |
| 2 | 月曜日 | 2 | Monday |
| 3 | 火曜日 | 3 | Tuesday |
| 4 | 水曜日 | 4 | Wednesday |
| 5 | 木曜日 | 5 | Thursday |
| 6 | 金曜日 | 6 | Friday |
| 7 | 土曜日 | 7 | Saturday |
| 8 | 休日 | 8 | holiday |
| 9 | 春 | 9 | spring |
| 10 | 夏 | 10 | summer |
| 11 | 秋 | 11 | fall |
| 12 | 冬 | 12 | winter |

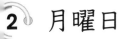

# Months／12か月

| 1 | 1月 | 1 | January |
| 2 | 2月 | 2 | February |
| 3 | 3月 | 3 | March |
| 4 | 4月 | 4 | April |
| 5 | 5月 | 5 | May |
| 6 | 6月 | 6 | June |
| 7 | 7月 | 7 | July |
| 8 | 8月 | 8 | August |
| 9 | 9月 | 9 | September |
| 10 | 10月 | 10 | October |
| 11 | 11月 | 11 | November |
| 12 | 12月 | 12 | December |

| | 日本語 | | 英語 |
|---|---|---|---|
| **1** | あか<br>赤 | **1** | red |
| **2** | あお<br>青 | **2** | blue |
| **3** | みどり<br>緑 | **3** | green |
| **4** | き<br>黄 | **4** | yellow |
| **5** | オレンジ色 | **5** | orange |
| **6** | ちゃ<br>茶 | **6** | brown |
| **7** | しろ<br>白 | **7** | white |
| **8** | ピンク | **8** | pink |
| **9** | むらさき<br>紫 | **9** | purple |
| **10** | くろ<br>黒 | **10** | black |
| **11** | グレー | **11** | gray |
| **12** | きん<br>金色 | **12** | gold |

| | 日本語 | | 英語 |
|---|---|---|---|
| 1 | 大きい | 1 | big |
| 2 | 小さい | 2 | small |
| 3 | 多い(多数の), たくさん | 3 | many |
| 4 | 多い(多量の), たくさん | 4 | much |
| 5 | 長い | 5 | long |
| 6 | 短い, 低い | 6 | short |
| 7 | (人や木が) 高い | 7 | tall |
| 8 | 太った | 8 | fat |
| 9 | 若い | 9 | young |
| 10 | 年とった, 古い | 10 | old |
| 11 | 重い | 11 | heavy |
| 12 | 軽い | 12 | light |

| 13 | 強い | 13 | strong |
| 14 | 弱い | 14 | weak |
| 15 | 良い | 15 | good |
| 16 | 悪い | 16 | bad |
| 17 | まちがった | 17 | wrong |
| 18 | 新しい | 18 | new |
| 19 | 左の | 19 | left |
| 20 | 右の，正しい | 20 | right |
| 21 | おなかがすいた | 21 | hungry |
| 22 | (おなかが) いっぱいの | 22 | full |
| 23 | のどがかわいた | 23 | thirsty |
| 24 | 金持ちの | 24 | rich |

| 25 | 美しい | 25 | beautiful |
| 26 | かわいい | 26 | pretty |
| 27 | きたない | 27 | dirty |
| 28 | 勇敢な<br>ゆう かん | 28 | brave |
| 29 | 親切な<br>しん せつ | 29 | kind |
| 30 | いそがしい | 30 | busy |
| 31 | まずしい | 31 | poor |
| 32 | 病気の | 32 | sick |
| 33 | 安い | 33 | cheap |
| 34 | (値段が) 高い<br>ね だん | 34 | expensive |
| 35 | きれいな | 35 | clean |
| 36 | 暗い | 36 | dark |

| 37 | うれしい | 37 | happy |
| 38 | 悲しい | 38 | sad |
| 39 | 怒った | 39 | angry |
| 40 | ねむい | 40 | sleepy |
| 41 | 疲れた | 41 | tired |
| 42 | さわがしい | 42 | noisy |
| 43 | おかしな，こっけいな | 43 | funny |
| 44 | こわい | 44 | scary |
| 45 | きびしい | 45 | strict |
| 46 | すてきな | 46 | nice |
| 47 | かんたんな | 47 | easy |
| 48 | むずかしい | 48 | difficult |

| # | 日本語 | 英語 |
|---|---|---|
| 1 | 早く | early |
| 2 | ゆっくり，おそく | slowly |
| 3 | 大声で | loudly |
| 4 | 注意深く | carefully |
| 5 | 一生けん命に | hard |
| 6 | 少しは | a little |
| 7 | ひとりで | alone |
| 8 | 決して〜でない | never |
| 9 | めったに〜しない | seldom |
| 10 | ふつうは | usually |
| 11 | とても，非常に | very |
| 12 | うまく，上手に | well |

| | 日本語 | | 英語 |
|---|---|---|---|
| **1** | お父さん，父 | **1** | father |
| **2** | お母さん，母 | **2** | mother |
| **3** | 兄 | **3** | big brother |
| **4** | 姉 | **4** | big sister |
| **5** | 弟 | **5** | little brother |
| **6** | 妹 | **6** | little sister |
| **7** | おじいさん，祖父 | **7** | grandfather |
| **8** | おばあさん，祖母 | **8** | grandmother |
| **9** | おじ | **9** | uncle |
| **10** | おば | **10** | aunt |
| **11** | いとこ | **11** | cousin |
| **12** | 子ども | **12** | child / children |

| | |
|---|---|
| **1** ネコ | **1** cat |
| **2** イヌ | **2** dog |
| **3** 鳥 | **3** bird |
| **4** ウシ（雌牛） | **4** cow |
| **5** アヒル | **5** duck |
| **6** サル | **6** monkey |
| **7** ウマ | **7** horse |
| **8** クマ | **8** bear |
| **9** ライオン | **9** lion |
| **10** トラ | **10** tiger |
| **11** ゾウ | **11** elephant |
| **12** カバ | **12** hippo |

| 13 | キツネ | 13 | fox |
| 14 | キリン | 14 | giraffe |
| 15 | カンガルー | 15 | kangaroo |
| 16 | ウサギ | 16 | rabbit |
| 17 | ヘビ | 17 | snake |
| 18 | クモ | 18 | spider |
| 19 | 恐竜 (きょうりゅう) | 19 | dinosaur |
| 20 | トカゲ | 20 | lizard |
| 21 | ヒツジ | 21 | sheep / sheep |
| 22 | ネズミ | 22 | mouse / mice |
| 23 | 魚 (さかな) | 23 | fish / fish |
| 24 | ガチョウ | 24 | goose / geese |

1 | 1
2 | 2
3 | 3
4 | 4
5 | 5
6 | 6
7 | 7
8 | 8
9 | 9
10 | 10
11 | 11
12 | 12

1 | one
2 | two
3 | three
4 | four
5 | five
6 | six
7 | seven
8 | eight
9 | nine
10 | ten
11 | eleven
12 | twelve

| 13 | 13 | | 13 | thirteen |
| 14 | 14 | | 14 | fourteen |
| 15 | 15 | | 15 | fifteen |
| 16 | 16 | | 16 | sixteen |
| 17 | 17 | | 17 | seventeen |
| 18 | 18 | | 18 | eighteen |
| 19 | 19 | | 19 | nineteen |
| 20 | 20 | | 20 | twenty |
| 21 | 30 | | 21 | thirty |
| 22 | 40 | | 22 | forty |
| 23 | 50 | | 23 | fifty |
| 24 | 60 | | 24 | sixty |

| 25 | 70 | 25 | seventy |
| 26 | 80 | 26 | eighty |
| 27 | 90 | 27 | ninety |
| 28 | 100 | 28 | one hundred |
| 29 | 1000 | 29 | one thousand |
| 30 | 1万 | 30 | ten thousand |
| 31 | 10万 | 31 | one hundred thousand |
| 32 | 100万 | 32 | one million |
| 33 | 1000万 | 33 | ten million |
| 34 | 1億 | 34 | one hundred million |
| 35 | 10億 | 35 | one billion |
| 36 | 100億 | 36 | ten billion |

Ordinal Numbers／序数

13

**1** 1番目の，最初の

**2** 2番目の

**3** 3番目の

**4** 4番目の

**5** 5番目の

**6** 6番目の

**7** 7番目の

**8** 8番目の

**9** 9番目の

**10** 10番目の

**11** 11番目の

**12** 12番目の

**1** first

**2** second

**3** third

**4** fourth

**5** fifth

**6** sixth

**7** seventh

**8** eighth

**9** ninth

**10** tenth

**11** eleventh

**12** twelfth

# Clothes／着る物

| | | | |
|---|---|---|---|
| **1** | ブラウス | **1** | blouse |
| **2** | 帽子, 野球帽<br>（ぼうし） | **2** | cap |
| **3** | 帽子（ふちあり）<br>（ぼうし） | **3** | hat |
| **4** | ズボン | **4** | pants |
| **5** | 運動ぐつ<br>（うんどう） | **5** | sneaker(s) |
| **6** | セーター | **6** | sweater |
| **7** | シャツ | **7** | shirt |
| **8** | くつ | **8** | shoe(s) |
| **9** | スカート | **9** | skirt |
| **10** | くつした | **10** | sock(s) |
| **11** | パジャマ | **11** | pajamas |
| **12** | レインコート | **12** | raincoat |

| | | | |
|---|---|---|---|
| 1 | 歯医者 | 1 | dentist |
| 2 | 医者 | 2 | doctor |
| 3 | 消防士 | 3 | firefighter |
| 4 | 看ご師 | 4 | nurse |
| 5 | 警察官 | 5 | police officer |
| 6 | 科学者 | 6 | scientist |
| 7 | 教師, 先生 | 7 | teacher |
| 8 | コック | 8 | cook |
| 9 | 事務員 | 9 | office clerk |
| 10 | 宇宙飛行士 | 10 | astronaut |
| 11 | サッカー選手 | 11 | soccer player |
| 12 | タクシー運転手 | 12 | taxi driver |

# Food／食べ物

| | | | |
|---|---|---|---|
| 1 | ケーキ | 1 | cake |
| 2 | フライドチキン | 2 | fried chicken |
| 3 | ハンバーガー | 3 | hamburger |
| 4 | スパゲティ | 4 | spaghetti |
| 5 | アイスクリーム | 5 | ice cream |
| 6 | パンケーキ | 6 | pancakes |
| 7 | パン | 7 | bread |
| 8 | ピザ | 8 | pizza |
| 9 | サラダ | 9 | salad |
| 10 | サンドイッチ | 10 | sandwich |
| 11 | 塩 | 11 | salt |
| 12 | さとう | 12 | sugar |

| | | |
|---|---|---|
| キャベツ | **1** | cabbage |
| にんじん | **2** | carrot |
| とうもろこし | **3** | corn |
| きゅうり | **4** | cucumber |
| レタス | **5** | lettuce |
| たまねぎ | **6** | onion |
| ピーマン | **7** | green pepper |
| かぼちゃ | **8** | pumpkin |
| トマト | **9** | tomato |
| じゃがいも | **10** | potato |
| ブロッコリー | **11** | broccoli |
| ホウレンソウ | **12** | spinach |

| | | | |
|---|---|---|---|
| 1 | リンゴ | 1 | apple |
| 2 | バナナ | 2 | banana |
| 3 | グレープフルーツ | 3 | grapefruit |
| 4 | ブドウ | 4 | grapes |
| 5 | メロン | 5 | melon |
| 6 | ミカン | 6 | orange |
| 7 | イチゴ | 7 | strawberry |
| 8 | パイナップル | 8 | pineapple |
| 9 | モモ | 9 | peach |
| 10 | スイカ | 10 | watermelon |
| 11 | ブルーベリー | 11 | blueberry |
| 12 | レモン | 12 | lemon |

# Drinks／飲み物

category
19

| | 日本語 | | 英語 |
|---|---|---|---|
| 1 | 牛乳 (ぎゅうにゅう) | 1 | milk |
| 2 | コーヒー | 2 | coffee |
| 3 | 紅茶 (こうちゃ) | 3 | tea |
| 4 | 緑茶 (りょくちゃ) | 4 | green tea |
| 5 | ジュース | 5 | juice |
| 6 | ワイン | 6 | wine |
| 7 | 水 | 7 | water |
| 8 | ビール | 8 | beer |
| 9 | ココア | 9 | hot chocolate |
| 10 | コーラ | 10 | cola |
| 11 | 炭酸飲料 (たんさんいんりょう) | 11 | pop |
| 12 | 清涼飲料水 (せいりょういんりょうすい) | 12 | soft drink |

| | | | |
|---|---|---|---|
| 1 | 野球 | 1 | baseball |
| 2 | バスケットボール | 2 | basketball |
| 3 | ドッジボール | 3 | dodgeball |
| 4 | サッカー | 4 | soccer |
| 5 | テニス | 5 | tennis |
| 6 | きかい体操 | 6 | gymnastics |
| 7 | スキー | 7 | skiing |
| 8 | スケート | 8 | skating |
| 9 | 水泳 | 9 | swimming |
| 10 | バレーボール | 10 | volleyball |
| 11 | 卓球 | 11 | table tennis |
| 12 | 陸上競技 | 12 | track |

| |  | |  |
|---|---|---|---|
| 1 | さんすう<br>算数 | 1 | math |
| 2 | りか<br>理科 | 2 | science |
| 3 | しゃかいか<br>社会科 | 3 | social studies |
| 4 | たいいく<br>体育 | 4 | P. E. |
| 5 | えいご<br>英語 | 5 | English |
| 6 | こくご<br>国語 | 6 | Japanese |
| 7 | ずこう<br>図工 | 7 | arts and crafts |
| 8 | かていか<br>家庭科 | 8 | home economics |
| 9 | おんがく<br>音楽 | 9 | music |
| 10 | ちょうれい<br>朝礼 | 10 | morning assembly |
| 11 | えんそく<br>遠足 | 11 | field trip |
| 12 | ほうかご<br>放課後 | 12 | after school |

| | |
|---|---|
| 1 本 | 1 book |
| 2 ノート | 2 notebook |
| 3 えんぴつ | 3 pencil |
| 4 消しゴム | 4 eraser |
| 5 じょうぎ | 5 ruler |
| 6 教科書 | 6 textbook |
| 7 紙 | 7 paper |
| 8 チョーク | 8 chalk |
| 9 はさみ | 9 scissors |
| 10 ホッチキス | 10 stapler |
| 11 ふでばこ | 11 pencil case |
| 12 シャープペンシル | 12 mechanical pencil |

| | | | |
|---|---|---|---|
| **1** | ブランコ | **1** | swing |
| **2** | てつぼう | **2** | horizontal bar |
| **3** | シーソー | **3** | seesaw |
| **4** | ジャングルジム | **4** | jungle gym |
| **5** | すべり台 | **5** | slide |
| **6** | うんてい | **6** | monkey bars |
| **7** | 体育館<br><small>たい いく かん</small> | **7** | gym |
| **8** | 旗<br><small>はた</small> | **8** | flag |
| **9** | 黒板<br><small>こく ばん</small> | **9** | blackboard |
| **10** | 小学校 | **10** | elementary school |
| **11** | 教室 | **11** | classroom |
| **12** | プール | **12** | swimming pool |

# In the Kitchen／台所にある物

| | | | |
|---|---|---|---|
| 1 | フライパン，（浅い）なべ | 1 | pan |
| 2 | スプーン | 2 | spoon |
| 3 | ナイフ | 3 | knife |
| 4 | さら 皿 | 4 | plate |
| 5 | なべ | 5 | pot |
| 6 | れいぞうこ 冷蔵庫 | 6 | fridge |
| 7 | オーブン | 7 | oven |
| 8 | こんろ，ガスレンジ | 8 | stove |
| 9 | フォーク | 9 | fork |
| 10 | トレー | 10 | tray |
| 11 | コップ | 11 | glass |
| 12 | すいはんき 炊飯器 | 12 | rice cooker |

| | | | |
|---|---|---|---|
| 1 | ソファ | 1 | sofa |
| 2 | ひじかけいす | 2 | armchair |
| 3 | テレビ | 3 | television |
| 4 | でん わ<br>電話 | 4 | telephone |
| 5 | テーブル | 5 | table |
| 6 | しん ぶん<br>新聞 | 6 | newspaper |
| 7 | カーテン | 7 | curtain |
| 8 | そうじ機<br>き | 8 | vacuum cleaner |
| 9 | まど<br>窓 | 9 | window |
| 10 | ドア | 10 | door |
| 11 | てん じょう<br>天井 | 11 | ceiling |
| 12 | かべ | 12 | wall |

| # | | # | |
|---|---|---|---|
| 1 | 机（つくえ） | 1 | desk |
| 2 | いす | 2 | chair |
| 3 | コンピューター | 3 | computer |
| 4 | テレビゲーム | 4 | video game |
| 5 | 電気スタンド, ランプ | 5 | lamp |
| 6 | 辞書（じしょ） | 6 | dictionary |
| 7 | 地図（ちず） | 7 | map |
| 8 | 雑誌（ざっし） | 8 | magazine |
| 9 | 通学用（つうがくよう）かばん | 9 | school bag |
| 10 | ベッド | 10 | bed |
| 11 | まくら | 11 | pillow |
| 12 | めざまし時計 | 12 | alarm clock |

# Body Parts／身体の部分

category 27

**1** 目（め）

**2** 鼻（はな）

**3** 口（くち）

**4** 耳（みみ）

**5** 顔（かお）

**6** 髪（かみ）

**7** 手（て）

**8** 指（ゆび）

**9** うで

**10** あし

**11** あし

**12** 歯（は）

**1** eye(s)

**2** nose

**3** mouth

**4** ear(s)

**5** face

**6** hair

**7** hand(s)

**8** finger(s)

**9** arm(s)

**10** leg(s)

**11** foot　feet

**12** tooth　teeth

forty-one 41

# Weather／天気・自然

| | 日本語 | | 英語 |
|---|---|---|---|
| **1** | 雨ふりの | **1** | rainy |
| **2** | 晴れた | **2** | fine |
| **3** | 日が照っている，天気のよい | **3** | sunny |
| **4** | 曇りの | **4** | cloudy |
| **5** | 風の強い | **5** | windy |
| **6** | 雪のふる | **6** | snowy |
| **7** | 寒い | **7** | cold |
| **8** | 暑い | **8** | hot |
| **9** | あたたかい | **9** | warm |
| **10** | すずしい | **10** | cool |
| **11** | むしむしした | **11** | humid |
| **12** | 地震 | **12** | earthquake |

**1** あめ 雨

**2** くも 雲

**3** ゆき 雪

**4** かぜ 風

**5** そら 空

**6** たいよう 太陽

**7** 月

**8** ほし 星

**9** 山

**10** 川

**11** 花

**12** 木

**1** rain

**2** cloud

**3** snow

**4** wind

**5** sky

**6** sun

**7** moon

**8** star

**9** mountain

**10** river

**11** flower

**12** tree

# Transportation／乗り物

| # | 日本語 | # | English |
|---|--------|---|---------|
| 1 | 自動車, くるま（じどうしゃ） | 1 | car |
| 2 | 自転車（じてんしゃ） | 2 | bicycle, bike |
| 3 | ジェット機（き） | 3 | jet |
| 4 | 飛行機（ひこうき） | 4 | airplane |
| 5 | ロケット | 5 | rocket |
| 6 | ボート | 6 | boat |
| 7 | 船（ふね） | 7 | ship |
| 8 | 電車（でんしゃ） | 8 | train |
| 9 | フェリー | 9 | ferry |
| 10 | バス | 10 | bus |
| 11 | 新幹線（しんかんせん） | 11 | bullet train |
| 12 | 地下鉄（ちかてつ） | 12 | subway |

| | 日本語 | | English |
|---|---|---|---|
| 1 | くうこう<br>空港 | 1 | airport |
| 2 | パン屋 | 2 | bakery |
| 3 | しやくしょ<br>市役所 | 3 | city hall |
| 4 | レストラン | 4 | restaurant |
| 5 | ぎんこう<br>銀行 | 5 | bank |
| 6 | スーパーマーケット | 6 | supermarket |
| 7 | アパート, マンション | 7 | apartment house |
| 8 | びょういん<br>病院 | 8 | hospital |
| 9 | としょかん<br>図書館 | 9 | library |
| 10 | こうえん<br>公園 | 10 | park |
| 11 | デパート | 11 | department store |
| 12 | ゆうびんきょく<br>郵便局 | 12 | post office |

| | 日本語 | | 英語 |
|---|---|---|---|
| **1** | ～の上に | **1** | on |
| **2** | ～の中に | **2** | in |
| **3** | ～の下に | **3** | under |
| **4** | ～のそばに | **4** | by |
| **5** | ～の前に | **5** | before |
| **6** | ～の後に | **6** | after |
| **7** | ～といっしょに | **7** | with |
| **8** | ～の間に | **8** | between |
| **9** | ～の正面に | **9** | in front of |
| **10** | ～できる | **10** | can |
| **11** | ～してもよい, ～かもしれない | **11** | may |
| **12** | ～しなければならない | **12** | have to |

| | | | |
|---|---|---|---|
| **1** | なに？ | **1** | what |
| **2** | どこ？ | **2** | where |
| **3** | いつ？ | **3** | when |
| **4** | だれ？ | **4** | who |
| **5** | だれの？ | **5** | whose |
| **6** | なぜ？ | **6** | why |
| **7** | どちら？ | **7** | which |
| **8** | どのように？ | **8** | how |
| **9** | なんじ？ | **9** | what time |
| **10** | いくつ（数）？ | **10** | how many |
| **11** | いくら（値段・量）？ | **11** | how much |
| **12** | なんさい（年齢）？ | **12** | how old |

# My Own Words List

1

2

3

4

5

6

7

8

9

10

11

12

1

2

3

4

5

6

7

8

9

10

11

12

13

14

15

16

17

18

19

20

21

22

23

24

13 _____

14 _____

15 _____

16 _____

17 _____

18 _____

19 _____

20 _____

21 _____

22 _____

23 _____

24 _____

# My Own Words List

25

26

27

28

29

30

31

32

33

34

35

36

25

26

27

28

29

30

31

32

33

34

35

36

37

38

39

40

41

42

43

44

45

46

47

48

37

38

39

40

41

42

43

44

45

46

47

48

# Japanese ▼ English

## 和英辞書
Japanese-English Dictionary

この「和英辞書」は、発信型英語教育のための和英辞書です。英語を学習している子供達が、知らないことばを簡単に調べ、「すぐに使うことができる」ことを目的としています。従来の英和辞書の画一的な観念を一新し、子供達の学習段階においては不必要と思われる言語学的に解説の複雑な語彙や表現については思い切って割愛し、子供達の視線に立って、知っている語彙を駆使して「自分の言いたいことを英語で言う」ことができるようにデザインしました。

すぐに使うことができるように、各語彙の後に発音記号をつけています。和英辞書を引く指針となる「見出しの日本語」の表記も、言いたいことばがすぐに見つけられるように、子供達が日頃使っている「言葉」にこだわって採用しました。

Children can check unfamiliar words in the Japanese-English Dictionary which provides sample sentences that help them understand how the words are actually used. 1,400+ words include the 564 basic words (pp.1-47), vocabulary children learn in school and additional words frequently used in their daily lives.

### 語 彙
児童英語教育に必須とされるカテゴリーごとの基本語彙564語 (pp.1-47の語彙)に加えて、小学校6年までに目に触れておきたい基本語彙および生活の中で頻繁に使う語彙、機能語を含めて約1,400語を抽出しました。

### 例 文
英語の使い方を示す例文は子供達が覚えやすく、そのまま使えるものを中心に適宜盛り込みました。

### つづり字
日本の英語教育で広く使われているアメリカ式を採用。英国式についてはここでは子供達の混乱を避けるためにあえて割愛しました。

### 発音記号
本辞書は、児童英語教育の特徴である「正しい発音の習得」を大切にするために、あえてカタカナを使わず、国際音標発音記号に沿って表記してあります。標準的な発音を掲げ、音声上の細かな違いについては割愛しました。アクセントは2音節以上の語彙には第1、第2アクセントを ´ ` で付し、1音節の語彙については学習者の読みやすさを考慮し、アクセント記号を省いてあります。

**表記上の補足**：不規則動詞の過去形、不規則名詞の複数形以外の変化形の記載については紙面の関係上省略しました。また、言語学的に解説が多く必要な語彙や表現、および、学習者が英語を「使う」にあたって決まりごとの多い語彙と、間投詞、固有名詞については紙面に限りがあるために割愛しました。

# あ ア

あいしている【（〜を）愛している】 **love** [lʌv]
→ あなたは私を愛していますか? *Do you love me?*

アイスクリーム **ice cream** [áis krì:m]

あいだ【（〜の）間】 **between** [bitwí:n]
　　　　　　 **during** [djúəriŋ] ＝〜ちゅう
　　● 冬休みの間 – during winter vacation

アイロンをかける **iron** [áiərn]
→ シャツにアイロンをかけなさい。 *Iron your shirt.*

あう【会う】 **meet** [mi:t] 過去形 met [met]
　　【会う】 **see** [si:] ＝みる 過去形 saw [sɔ:]
→ また明日会おうね。 *See you tomorrow.*

あお【青】 **blue** [blu:]

あか【赤】 **red** [red]

あがる【上がる】 **rise** [raiz] ＝のぼる 過去形 rose [rouz]

あかり **light** [lait] ＝あかるい, でんとう, かるい

あかるい【明るい】 **light** [lait] ⇔ dark [dɑːrk] 暗い
　　　　　【明るい】 **bright** [brait] ＝あたまがよい

あき【秋】 **fall** [fɔ:l] ＝おちる

あける【開ける】 **open** [oupn]

あげる **give** [giv] ＝くれる, ください 過去形 gave [geiv]
→ これ, きみにあげる。 *I'll give this to you.*
　　● えさをあげる ＝ feed

あご **chin** [tʃin]

あさ【朝】 **morning** [mɔ́:rniŋ]

あさごはん【朝ごはん】 **breakfast** [brékfəst]

あし【足】 **foot** [fut] 複数形 feet [fi:t]（足首からつま先を言う）
　　　 **leg(s)** [leg(z)]（太ももから足首までを言う）
→ 私は歩いて学校へ行きます。 *I go to school on foot.*

あじがする【味がする】 **taste** [teist]

あしのゆび【足の指】 **toe** [tou]

あした【明日】 **tomorrow** [təmárou]

あそぶ【遊ぶ】 **play** [plei] ＝（〜を）する, （〜を）ひく
→ テレビゲームをしよう。 *Let's play video games.*
→ 車の多い通りで遊んではいけません。 *Don't play on busy streets.*

あたえる【（〜を）与える】 **give** [giv] 過去形 gave [geiv]
　　＝あげる, くれる, ください

あたたかい【暖かい】 **warm** [wɔ:rm]

あたま【頭】 **head** [hed] ● 頭痛 ＝ headache [hédèik]

→ 私は頭がいたい。 *I have a headache.*

あたまがよい【頭が良い】 **bright** [brait] ＝あかるい

あたらしい【新しい】 **new** [nju:] ⇔ old [ould] 古い

あちら **over there** [óuvər ðeər]（場所を表す） ＝むこうに
　　　 **that way** [ðæt wei]（方向を表す）

あつい【暑い】 **hot** [hat] ⇔ cold [kould] 寒い

あつい【熱い】 **hot** [hat] ● 温泉 ＝ hot spring

あつい【厚い】 **thick** [θik] ⇔ thin [θin] うすい

アップルパイ **apple pie** [ǽpl pài]

あつめる【集める】 **collect** [kəlékt]

あてさき【あて先】 **address** [ədrés] ＝じゅうしょ

あとに【（〜の）後に】 **after** [ǽftər], **later** [léitər]
→ 夕食の後に宿題をします。 *I do my homework after dinner.* ● お先にどうぞ。 ＝ After you.
→ あとでね。 *See you later.*

あなたの **your** [juər]
→ あなたのノートを見せてください。 *Please show me your notebook.*

あなたは（が） **you** [ju:]
→ あなたは先生ですか? *Are you a teacher?*

あなたを（に） **you** [ju:]
→ 私はあなたを愛しています。 *I love you.*

あに【兄】 **big brother** [bíg brʌðər] ＝ older brother

あね【姉】 **big sister** [bíg sistər] ＝ older sister

あの **that** [ðæt, ðət] ＝あちら, あれ
→ あの男の人は私達の英語の先生です。
*That man is our English teacher.*
　　● 2つ以上の物をさす時は those [ðouz]

アパート **apartment house** [əpá:rtmənt hàus]
　　＝マンション

アヒル **duck** [dʌk]

あまりにも… **too** [tu:] ＝〜もまた

あめ【雨】 **rain** [rein]
→ 日本では6月に雨がよく降ります。 *In Japan, we have a lot of rain in June.*

あめがふる【雨が降る】 **rain** [rein]
→ 明日は雨でしょう。 *It will rain tomorrow.*

あめふりの【雨降りの】 **rainy** [réini]
→ 今日は雨です。 *It's rainy today.*
→ 雨の日は好きですか? *Do you like rainy days?*

アメリカンフットボール **football** [fútbɔ̀:l]

1

あ
い

**あらう**〔（〜を）洗う〕 **wash** [waʃ]

→ せっけんで手を洗いなさい。このタオルでふきなさい。 *Wash your hands with soap.  Dry your hands with this towel.*

● 皿を洗う＝wash the dishes（do the dishes とも言う）

● 洗濯をする＝wash the clothes

**アリ　ant** [ænt]

**ありがとう　thank** [θæŋk]　＝かんしゃする

→ 助けてくれてありがとう。 *Thank you for your help.* どういたしまして。 *You're welcome.* （目上の人やていねいに言う時）*My pleasure.*

**あるく**〔歩く〕 **walk** [wɔːk]

→ 私は歩いて学校に行きます。 *I walk to school.*

**アルバム　album** [ælbəm]

**アルファベット　alphabet** [ælfəbèt]

**あれ　that** [ðæt, ðət]　＝あちら，あの

→ あれを見せてください。 *Please show me that.*

**あれら　those** [ðouz]　　that の複数形

**あわ**〔泡〕 **bubble** [bʌbl]　＝しゃぼんだま

**あんぜんな**〔安全な〕 **safe** [seif]　＝きんこ

⇔ dangerous [déindʒərəs] 危険な

## い　イ

**いいあてる　guess** [ges]　＝おもう，すいそくする

**いいえ　no** [nou]　＝（なにも）ない

**イーメール**〔eメール〕 **e-mail** [íː meil]

**いう**〔言う〕 **say** [sei]　過去形 **said** [sed]

→ 「こんにちは」は英語で何と言いますか？ *How do you say "Konnichiwa" in English?*

**いえ**〔家〕 **house** [haus]　● home は家庭生活としての場（家），house は建物としての意味が含まれます。

**いきて**〔生きて〕 **alive** [əláiv]

→ 彼は生きている。 *He is alive.*

**いく**〔行く〕 **go** [gou]　過去形 **went** [went]

→ 私は弟と一緒に学校に行きます。 *I go to school with my little brother.*

**いくつ**（数） **how many** [hau méni]

→ 1週間は何日ありますか？ *How many days are there in a week?*

**いくつかの　some** [sʌm], **any** [éni]　● any は否

定文で「少しも〜ない」という意味になります。

**いくら**（値段・量） **how much** [hau mʌtʃ]

→ この辞書はいくらですか？ *How much is this dictionary?*

**いけ**〔池〕 **pond** [pɑnd]

**いしゃ**〔医者〕 **doctor** [dɑ́ktər]

→ 医者にかかったほうがいいですよ。 *You should see a doctor.*

**いじわるな**〔意地悪な〕 **mean** [miːn], **rude** [ruːd]

→ 私に意地悪な態度をしないで。 *Don't be rude to me.*

**いす**〔椅子〕 **chair** [tʃeər]　● 議長＝chair person

**いそがしい**〔忙しい〕 **busy** [bízi]

→ 私は1日中忙しい。 *I'm busy all day long.*

→ 電話が話し中です。 *The line is busy.*

**いそぐ**〔急ぐ〕 **hurry** [hə́ːri]

→ 急いで！ *Hurry up!*

**いちがつ**〔1月〕 **January** [dʒǽnjuəri]

→ 1年の最初の月は1月です。 *The first month of the year is January.*

**イチゴ　strawberry** [strɔ́ːbèri]

**いちにち**〔1日〕 **one day** [wʌn dei]

**いちにちじゅう**〔1日中〕 **all day** [ɔːl dei]

→ 私は1日中勉強した。 *I studied all day (long).*

**いちねん**〔1年〕 **one year** [wʌn jiər]

**いちばんよい**〔一番良い〕 **best** [best]

**いつ　when** [hwen]

→ あなたの誕生日はいつですか？ *When is your birthday?*

**いっかげつ**〔1か月〕 **one month** [wʌn mʌnθ]　＝つき

**いっしゅうかん**〔1週間〕 **one week** [wʌn wiːk]＝しゅ

→ 1週間は7日です。 *One week has seven days*

→ 私は東京に1週間滞在していました。 *I stayed in Tokyo for a week.*

**いっしょに**〔一緒に〕 **with** [wið], **together** [təgéðər

→ 私は友達と一緒に学校に来ます。 *I come to school with my friends.*

→ 一緒に行きましょう。 *Let's go together.*

**いっしょうけんめいに**〔一生懸命に〕 **hard** [hɑːrd]　＝かたい，むずかしい

→ 一生懸命に英語を勉強しなさい。 *Study English hard*

いっぱいの **full** [ful] ⇔ empty [émpti] からの
→ 私はおなかがいっぱいです。 *I am full.*

いつもは **usually** [júːʒuəli] ＝ふつうは

いとこ **cousin** [kʌ́zn]

いなくてさびしい【いなくて寂しい】 **miss** [mis] ＝〜しそこなう
→ あなたがいなくて寂しいです。 *I miss you.*

イヌ **dog** [dɔːg] （鳴き声は bow wow） ● 子犬＝puppy

いのち【命】 **life** [laif] ＝せいかつ

いま【今】 **now** [nau]

いま【居間】 **living room** [líviŋ ruːm]

いみする【意味する】 **mean** [miːn] ＝いじわるな
過去形 meant [ment] ※発音注意

いもうと【妹】 **little sister** [lítl sistər]
＝younger sister

イモムシ **caterpillar** [kǽtərpìlər] ＝けむし

いりぐち【入口】 **entrance** [éntrəns]

いる【（家族や友達が）いる】 **have** [hæv, həv]
＝もっている，（ペットを）かう 過去形 had [hæd, həd]
→ 私には3人の姉がいます。 *I have three older sisters.*

いれる【入れる】 **put** [put] 過去形 put [put]， **let... in**
→ 鉛筆をふでばこに入れなさい。 *Put your pencil in your pencil case.*
→ 中に入れて。 *Let me in.*

いろ【色】 **color** [kʌ́lər]

## う ウ

うえに【（〜の）上に】 **on** [ɑn]

うけとる【受け取る】 **get** [get]， **receive** [risíːv]

うごく【動く】 **move** [muːv] ＝ひっこす，かんどうする

ウサギ **rabbit** [rǽbit]

ウシ【雌牛（めうし）】 **cow** [kau] ● 雄牛（おうし）＝ox [ɑks]
● ジュゴンは sea cow と言います。

うしろ【後ろ（の）】 **back** [bæk] ＝せなか

うそ（をつく）【嘘（をつく）】 **lie** [lai] ＝よこになる
→ 嘘をつかないでよ。 *Don't tell me a lie.*

うた【歌】 **song** [sɔːŋ]

うたう【歌う】 **sing** [siŋ] 過去形 sang [sæŋ]

うちゅう【宇宙】 **space** [speis]， **the universe** [júːnivə̀ːrs]

うちゅうひこうし【宇宙飛行士】 **astronaut** [ǽstrənɔ̀ːt]

うつ【打つ】 **hit** [hit] 過去形 hit [hit] ＝まかす

うつくしい【美しい】 **beautiful** [bjúːtifəl]

うで【腕】 **arm(s)** [ɑːrm(z)] ● 武器という意味もあります。

うでどけい【腕時計】 **watch** [wɑtʃ]

ウマ **horse** [hɔːrs] ● 鳴き声は neigh neigh [nei]

うまれる【生まれる】 **born** [bɔːrn]
→ 私は1998年生まれです。 *I was born in 1998.*

うみ【海】 **sea** [siː]， **ocean** [óuʃən]

うる【（〜を）売る】 **sell** [sel] 過去形 sold [sould]

うるさい **noisy** [nɔ́izi] ＝さわがしい

うれしい **happy** [hǽpi]， **glad** [glæd]

うんてい **monkey bars** [mʌ́ŋki bɑːrz]

うんてんする【運転する】 **drive** [draiv] 過去形 drove [drouv]
→ 免許なしに運転することはできません。 *We cannot drive a car without a driver's license.*

うんどうぐつ【運動ぐつ】 **sneaker(s)** [sníːkər(z)]

うんどうじょう【運動場】 **playground** [pléigràund]
→ 運動場で遊ぼう。 *Let's play on the playground.*

うんどうする【運動する】 **exercise** [éksərsàiz]

## え エ

え【絵】 **picture** [píktʃər] ＝しゃしん

えいが【映画】 **movie** [múːvi]

えいご【英語】 **English** [íŋgliʃ]
→ あなたは英語を話せますか？ *Can you speak English?*

えがく【（〜を）描く】 **draw** [drɔː] 過去形 drew [druː]

えさをあたえる **feed** [fiːd] 過去形 fed [fed]
→ ペットにえさを与えて。 *Feed the pet.*

エスカレーター **escalator** [éskəlèitər]

えらぶ【選ぶ】 **choose** [tʃuːz] 過去形 chose [tʃouz]

エレベーター **elevator** [élivèitər]

えんそく【遠足】 **field trip** [fíːld trip]
→ 私たちは昨日遠足で動物園に行きました。 *We went on a field trip to the zoo yesterday.*

えんとつ【煙突】 **chimney** [tʃímni]

えんぴつ【鉛筆】 **pencil** [pénsəl]
● シャープペンシル＝mechanical pencil（英語でシャープペンシルとは言わない）
● 鉛筆けずり＝pencil sharpener

# お オ

おい〖甥〗 **nephew** [néfjuː]

おいしい　**delicious** [dilíʃəs], **good** [gud]
→ このパイはとてもおいしい。　*This pie is delicious.*
→ このパイはおいしそうなにおいがする。　*This pie smells good.*

おえる〖終える〗 **finish** [fíniʃ]

おおい〖多い〗 **many** [méni] （数えられる物） ＝たすうの
**much** [mʌtʃ] （数えられない物） ＝たりょうの

おおきい〖大きい〗 **big** [big]　⇔ little, small
**large** [laːrdʒ]
→ もう，大きくなったのね（なったのだから）。　*You are a big boy (girl) now.*

おおごえで〖大声で〗 **loudly** [láudli]
→ もっと大きな声で話しなさい。　*Speak more loudly.*

オートバイ　**motorcycle** [móutərsàikl]
**motorbike** [móutərbàik]

オーブン　**oven** [ʌ́vn]

おかあさん〖お母さん〗 **mother** [mʌ́ðər]　＝はは

おかしな〖可笑しな〗 **funny** [fʌ́ni] ＝こっけいな，おもしろい

おきる〖起きる〗 **get up** [get ʌp] 過去形 got up
→ いつも私は7時30分に起きます。　*I usually get up at seven thirty.*

おく〖置く〗 **set** [set] ＝セットする 過去形 set [set]（同形）
◉ 食卓の準備をする＝set the table

おくる〖（〜を）送る〗 **send** [send] 過去形 sent [sent]
→ 私は祖母に手紙を送りました。　*I sent a letter to my grandmother.*

おこった〖怒った〗 **angry** [ǽŋgri] ◉怒る＝get angry
→ 彼はすぐに怒る。　*He gets angry easily.*

おこる〖起こる〗 **happen** [hǽpən]

おじ　**uncle** [ʌ́ŋkl]

おじいさん　**grandfather** [grǽnfàːðər] ＝そふ

おしいれ〖押入れ〗 **closet** [klázit] ＝とだな

おしえる　**teach** [tiːtʃ] 過去形 taught [tɔːt]
**tell** [tel] 過去形 told [tould]（言う，話す）
**show** [ʃou]（示す，見せる）
→ あなたの家族のことを教えてください。　*Please tell me about your family.*
→ 図書館への行き方を教えてください。　*Please show me the way to the library.*

おす〖押す〗 **push** [puʃ]
→ 押さないでください。　*Don't push me.*

おそい〖遅い〗 **late** [leit]（時間が遅い）　⇔ early
〖遅い〗 **slow** [slou]（速度が遅い）　⇔ fast
→ 私は学校に遅刻しました。遅れてごめんなさい。　*I was late for school. I'm sorry I am late.*

おちる〖落ちる〗 **fall** [fɔːl] 過去形 fell [fel] ＝あき
〖落ちる〗 **fail** [feil]（試験に）, **drop** [drɑp]（しずくが）

おっと〖夫〗 **husband** [hʌ́zbənd]

おてあらい〖お手洗い〗 **bathroom** [bǽθrùːm] ＝ふろば

おと〖音〗 **sound** [saund]

おとうさん〖お父さん〗 **father** [fáːðər] ＝ちち

おとうと〖弟〗 **little brother** [lítl brʌ́ðər]
＝ younger brother

おとこのこ〖男の子〗 **boy** [bɔi] ＝だんし

おとこのひと〖男の人〗 **man** [mæn] ＝にんげん
複数形 （2人以上の男の人は） men [men]

おとずれる〖訪れる〗 **visit** [vízit] ＝ほうもんする

おどる〖踊る〗 **dance** [dæns]

おどろく〖驚く〗 **be surprised (at)...** ＝びっくりする

おなか〖お腹〗 **belly** [béli]　◉ おへそ＝bellybutton

おなかがすいた　**hungry** [hʌ́ngri]　⇔ full
→ 私たちはおなかがすいています。　*We are hungry.*

おば　**aunt** [ænt]

おばあさん　**grandmother** [grǽnmʌ̀ðər] ＝そぼ

おばけ〖お化け〗 **ghost** [goust] ＝ゆうれい

おばけやしき〖お化け屋敷〗 **haunted house** [hɔ́ːntid hàus]

おぼえている〖（〜を）覚えている〗 **remember** [rimémbər]
→ 彼の名前を覚えていますか？ *Do you remember his name?*

おもい〖重い〗 **heavy** [hévi]　⇔ light

おもう〖思う〗 **think** [θiŋk] 過去形 thought [θɔːt] ＝かんがえる
〖思う〗 **guess** [ges] ＝いいあてる，すいそくする

おもさをはかる〖重さを計る，重さが〜ある〗 **weigh** [wei]

おもしろい　**interesting** [íntəristiŋ]（興味がある）
**funny** [fʌ́ni]（おかしな，こっけいな）
**exciting** [iksáitiŋ]（わくわくするような）

おもちゃ　**toy** [tɔi]

おや〖親〗 **parent** [péərənt] ◉ 両親＝parents

おやゆび〖親指〗 **thumb** [θʌm]

およぐ【泳ぐ】 **swim** [swim]　過去形 swam [swæm]
→ 私は平泳ぎで上手に泳げるよ。 *I can swim breast stroke well.* ● 平泳ぎ= breast stroke

およそ **about** [əbáut]　=〜について, やく

おりる【降りる】 **get off...** [get ɔf]　過去形 got [gat] off
【下りる】 **go down** [gou daun]
● 電車から降りる= get off the train
→ 階段をおりなさい。 *Go downstairs.*

オレンジいろ **orange** [ɔ́:rindʒ]

オレンジジュース **orange juice** [ɔ́:rindʒ dʒùːs]

おわる【終わる】 **finish** [fíniʃ], **end** [end] **be over** [bi óuvər]
→ 終わったよ。 *I'm finished.*
→ 時間が来ました。レッスンは終わりです。 *Time is up. The lesson is over.*

おんがく【音楽】 **music** [mjúːzik]

おんなのこ【女の子】 **girl** [gə:rl]　=じょし

おんなのひと【女の人】 **lady** [léidi], **woman** [wúmən]
複数形 (2人以上の女の人は) women [wímin]

# か　カ

か【蚊】 **mosquito** [məskíːtou]
→ 蚊に刺された。 *A mosquito bit me.*

〜がある **there** [ðeər, ðər]　=そこに

カーテン **curtain** [kə́:rtən]
→ カーテンを閉めてください。 *Please draw the curtains together.*

かい【会】 **meeting** [míːtiŋ]

かいがい【海外】 **overseas** [òuvərsíːz]
● 海外旅行= travel overseas または travel abroad

かいけつする【解決する】 **solve** [salv]

がいこくの【外国の】 **foreign** [fɔ́:rin]
● 外国語= foreign language

かいしゃ【会社】 **company** [kʌ́mpəni]

がいしゅつしている【外出している】 **be out** [bi aut]
= るすにする

かいぶつ【怪物】 **monster** [mánstər]　=モンスター

かいものにいく【買い物に行く】 **go shopping** [ʃápiŋ]
→ 買い物に行きましょう。 *Let's go shopping.*

かう【買う】 **buy** [bai]　過去形 bought [bɔːt]

【飼う】 **have** [hæv, həv]　過去形 had [hæd, həd]
→ 私はあの店でこのカバンを買いました。 *I bought this bag at that store.*
● 食料品を買う= buy groceries
→ 私は犬を3匹飼っています。 *I have three dogs.*

かえる【変える】 **change** [tʃeindʒ]

かえる【帰る】 **go back** [gou bæk], **come back** [kʌm bæk]

かお【顔】 **face** [feis]
→ 面と向かって話をしよう。 *Let's talk face to face.*

かがくしゃ【科学者】 **scientist** [sáiəntist]
→ 私は科学者になりたい。 *I want to be a scientist.*

かがやく【輝く】 **shine** [ʃain]　過去形 shone [ʃoun]

かかる **take** [teik]　=とる, もっていく
→ 学校へ行くのに5分かかる。 *It takes me five minutes to go to school.*

かぎ【鍵】 **key** [kiː]
→ このカギでドアを開けてください。 *Please unlock the door with this key.*

かく【書く】 **write** [rait]　過去形 wrote [rout]
【描く】 **paint** [peint] (色をぬる)
【書く】 **draw** [drɔː] (線で書く)　過去形 drew [druː]
→ 英語で名前が書けますか? *Can you write your name in English?*
→ 答えを線で書きなさい。 *Draw lines to the correct answers.*

がくせい【学生】 **student** [stjúːdənt]　=せいと

がくねん【学年】 **grade** [greid]　=せいせき
→ 私は5年生です。 *I am in the fifth grade.*

かくれる【隠れる】 **hide** [haid]　過去形 hid [hid]

かくれんぼ **hide-and-seek** [háidənsíːk]
→ かくれんぼしようよ。誰がオニになる? *Let's play hide-and-seek. Who wants to be IT?* (IT=オニ)

かけざん【掛け算】 **...times...is...**
→ 5×3=15 *Five times three is fifteen.*

かける **hang** [hæŋ]　=つるす, ぶらさがる
**call** [kɔːl] (電話をかける)
**wear** [weər] (めがねをかける)
→ このカレンダーを壁にかけなさい。 *Hang this calendar on the wall.*
→ 後で電話をかけます。 *I'll call you later.*
→ 彼はめがねをかけている。 *He is wearing glasses.*

か

かこ【過去】 **past** [pæst, pɑːst]

かご　**basket** [bǽskit]　● 鳥かご＝cage [keidʒ]

かさ【傘】 **umbrella** [ʌmbrélə]

➡ かさを必ず持って行きなさい。　*Be sure to take an umbrella with you.*

かざん【火山】 **volcano** [vɑlkéinou]

かしゅ【歌手】 **singer** [síŋər]

かす【貸す】 **lend** [lend]　過去形 lent [lent]

➡ 自転車を貸してくれませんか？　*Will you lend me your bike?*

● 持ち運びができないものの貸し借りには lend は使わない。

トイレを借りる時→May I use the bathroom?

電話を借りる時→May I use your telephone?

かず【数】 **number** [nʌ́mbər]　＝ばんごう

ガスレンジ　**stove** [stouv]　＝レンジ

かぜ【風】 **wind** [wind]

● そよ風は breeze, あらしは storm と言います。

かぜのつよい【風の強い】 **windy** [wíndi]

➡ 今日は風が強いです。　*It's windy today.*

かぞえる【数える】 **count** [kaunt]

➡ 君のことを当てにしてもいい？　*Can I count on you?*

● ～を当てにする＝count on...

かぞく【家族】 **family** [fǽməli]

かた【肩】 **shoulder** [ʃóuldər]

かたい【硬い】 **hard** [háːrd]　⇔soft やわらかい

＝いっしょうけんめいに, むずかしい

➡ このクッキーは硬すぎるよ。　*This cookie is too hard.*

かたづける【片付ける】 **put away** [pút əwèi]

➡ かばんに本をしまいなさい。　*Put your book away in your bag.*

かだん【花壇】 **flower bed** [fláuər bèd]

ガチョウ　**goose** [guːs]　複数形 geese [giːs]

かつ【勝つ】 **win** [win]　過去形 won [wʌn]

がっこう【学校】 **school** [skuːl]

➡ 我々は勉強するために学校に行きます。　*We go to school to study.*

かていか【家庭科】 **home economics** [houm ìːkənámiks]

かなしい【悲しい】 **sad** [sæd]

かなづち　**hammer** [hǽmər]　＝ハンマー

かね【鐘】 **bell** [bel]　＝すず, ベル

かね【金】 **money** [mʌ́ni]

かねもちの【金持ちの】 **rich** [ritʃ]　⇔poor まずしい

かのじょたちの【彼女達の】 **their** [ðeər, ðər]　＝かれらの

➡ 彼女達のお母さんを知っています。　*I know their mother.*

かのじょたちは(が)【彼女達は(が)】 **they** [ðei]　＝かれらは(が)

➡ 彼女達は姉妹です。　*They are sisters.*

かのじょたちを(に)【彼女達を(に)】 **them** [ðəm]　＝かれらを(に)

➡ 彼女達にノートを見せてあげてください。　*Show them your notebook.*

かのじょは(が)【彼女は(が)】 **she** [ʃiː]

➡ 彼女はパイロットです。　*She is a pilot.*

かのじょを(に), ～の【彼女を(に), ～の】 **her** [hər]

➡ 彼女の名前はみさきです。　*Her name is Misaki.*

➡ 私は彼女のEメールアドレスを知りません。　*I don't know her e-mail address.*

カバ　**hippo** [hípou]　＝hippopotamus [hipəpátəms

かべ【壁】 **wall** [wɔːl]

かぼちゃ　**pumpkin** [pʌ́mpkin]

かみ【髪】 **hair** [heər]

➡ ぼくはあの床屋で髪を切りました。　*I had my hair cut at that barber.*

かみ【紙】 **paper** [péipər]

➡ 紙を1枚もらえませんか？　*Can I have a piece of paper, please?*

かみなり　**thunder** [θʌ́ndər]（ゴロゴロと鳴る音） **lightning** [láitniŋ]（いなずま, 光）

かむ【噛む】 **bite** [bait]　過去形 bit [bit]

➡ 犬に指をかまれた。　*The dog bit my fingers.*

➡ 一口ちょうだい。　*Can I have a bite?*

カメラ　**camera** [kǽmərə]

かもく【科目】 **school subjects** [skúːl sʌ̀bdʒikts]　＝きょう

かもしれない　**may** [mei]（推量を表す）　＝してもよい

➡ 今日の午後雨が降るかもしれません。　*It may rain this afternoon.*

かゆい **itchy** [ítʃi]

➡ 背中がかゆい。　*My back is itchy.*

かようび【火曜日】 **Tuesday** [tjúːzdei]

からだ【身体】 **body** [bádi]

からの【空の】 **empty** [émpti]　＝なかみのない　⇔ful

➡ この席は空いています。　*This seat is empty.*

からにする【空にする】 **empty** [émpti]

◎ ごみ箱をからにする ＝ empty the dust box

かりる【借りる】 **borrow** [bárou], **rent** [rent], **use** [ju:z]

◎ 一時的に借りる場合は borrow を使う。

➡ 2000円お借りしてもいいですか？ *May I borrow two thousand yen?*

◎ お金を出して部屋などを借りる場合は rent を使う。

➡ 車を借りよう。 *Let's rent a car.*

◎ トイレや電話は「使わせてください」の意味で use を使う。

➡ トイレを借りてもいい？ *Can I use the bathroom?*

かるい【軽い】 **light** [lait] ⇔ **heavy** [hévi] 重い

かれの【彼の】 **his** [hiz]

➡ 彼の名前はてつやです。 *His name is Tetsuya.*

かれは（が）【彼は（が）】 **he** [hi:, hi]

➡ 彼はお医者さんです。 *He is a doctor.*

かれを（に）【彼を（に）】 **him** [him]

➡ あなたは彼を知っていますか？ *Do you know him?*

ガレージ **garage** [gərá:dʒ]

➡ ガレージに駐車してください。 *Park your car in the garage.*

かれらの【彼らの】 **their** [ðeər, ðər] ＝かのじょたちの

➡ 私は彼らのお母さんを知っています。 *I know their mother.*

かれらは（が）【彼らは（が）】 **they** [ðei] ＝かのじょたちは（が）

➡ 彼らは私の友だちです。 *They are my friends.*

かれらを（に）【彼らを（に）】 **them** [ðəm] ＝かのじょたちを（に）

➡ あなたのノートを彼らに見せてあげて。 *Show them your notebook.*

カレンダー **calendar** [kǽləndər]

かわ【川】 **river** [rívər]

➡ この町には大きな川が流れています。 *A big river runs through this town.*

かわいい **pretty** [príti], **cute** [kju:t], **lovely** [lʌ́vli]

かわいた【乾いた】 **dry** [drai] ⇔ **wet** [wet] ぬれた

かわかす【乾かす】 **dry** [drai]

かん【缶】 **can** [kæn] ＝～できる

かんがえる【考える】 **think** [θiŋk] 過去形 **thought** [θɔːt]

➡ 今考え中です。 *I'm thinking now.*

カンガルー **kangaroo** [kæŋgərúː]

かんごし【看護師】 **nurse** [nəːrs]

かんしゃする【感謝する】 **thank** [θæŋk] ＝ありがとう

かんじる【感じる】 **feel** [fiːl] 過去形 **felt** [felt]

➡ 気分が悪い。 *I feel sick.*

➡ めまいがする。 *I feel dizzy.*

かんたんな【簡単な】 **easy** [íːzi], **simple** [simpl]

➡ これは簡単です。 *This is easy.*

かんどうする【感動する】 **move** [muːv] ＝うごく、ひっこす

カンニングをする **cheat** [tʃiːt] ＝だます

# き キ

き【木】 **tree** [triː] ◎ 丸太 ＝ log ◎ 材木 ＝ wood

きいろ【黄色】 **yellow** [jélou]

きかい【機会】 **chance** [tʃæns]

きかいたいそう【きかい体操】 **gymnastics** [dʒimnǽstiks]

きく【聞く】 **listen** [lisn] ◎（～の言うことを）聞く ＝ listen to... **ask** [æsk] ＝たずねる、たのむ

➡（私の言うことを）聞きなさい。 *Listen to me.*

➡ どんなことでも聞いてください。 *You can ask me any questions.*

きく, きこえる【聞く, 聞こえる】 **hear** [hiər]
過去形 **heard** [həːrd] ※発音注意

➡ 聞こえますか？ *Can you hear me?*

きけん【危険】 **danger** [déindʒər]

きけんな【危険な】 **dangerous** [déindʒərəs] ⇔ safe

➡ ～するのは危険だ。 *It is dangerous to...*

きずつく【傷つく】 **hurt** [həːrt] 過去形 **hurt** [həːrt]（同形） ＝けがをする

きせつ【季節】 **season** [síːzn]

きた【北】 **north** [nɔːrθ]

ギター **guitar** [gitár]

きたいする【期待する】 **hope** [houp] ＝のぞむ、ねがう

きたえる【鍛える】 **train** [trein]

きたない【汚い】 **dirty** [də́ːrti] ⇔ **clean** きれいな

きつい **tight** [tait]

➡ このシャツは私にはきつい。 *This shirt is too tight for me.*

キツネ **fox** [faks]

きっぷ【切符】 **ticket** [tíkit] ＝チケット

きている【(服を)着ている】 **wear** [weər] 過去形 **wore** [wɔːr]

➡ 彼女は今日～を着ている。 *She is wearing... today.*

きのう【昨日】 **yesterday** [jéstərdei]

きびしい【厳しい】 **strict** [strict]

→ ぼくたちの新しい先生はとてもきびしい。 *Our new teacher is very strict.*

きめる【決める】 **decide** [disáid]

きもちいい **comfortable** [kʌ́mfərtəbl]

きゃく【客】 **guest** [gest]

キャッチボールをする **play catch** [plèi kǽtʃ]

→ キャッチボールしようよ。 *Let's play catch.*

キャベツ **cabbage** [kǽbidʒ]

◉ モンシロチョウ＝cabbage butterfly [bʌ́tərflài]

きゅうか【休暇】 **vacation** [veikéiʃən] ＝やすみ

きゅうけい【休憩】 **rest** [rest] ＝やすみ　◉ breakとも言う

きゅうこう【急行】 **express** [iksprés] ＝そくたつ

きゅうじつ【休日】 **holiday** [hɑ́lədèi] ＝さいじつ

きゅうに【急に】 **suddenly** [sʌ́dnli] ＝とつぜん

ぎゅうにゅう【牛乳】 **milk** [milk]

きゅうり **cucumber** [kjúːkʌmbər]

→ きゅうりを輪切りにしなさい。 *Cut the cucumber in round slices.* ◉ sea cucumberはナマコの意味。

きょう【今日】 **today** [tədéi]

きょうか【教科】 **school subjects** [skúːl sʌbʒikts] ＝かもく

きょうかい【教会】 **church** [tʃəːrtʃ]

きょうかしょ【教科書】 **textbook** [tékstbuk]

きょうし【教師】 **teacher** [tíːtʃər] ＝せんせい

きょうしつ【教室】 **classroom** [klǽsruːm]

きょうみがある【興味がある】 **interested** [íntəristəd]

→ 私は科学に興味があります。 *I am interested in science.*

きょうりゅう【恐竜】 **dinosaur** [dáinəsɔ̀ːr]

きょねん【去年】 **last year** [lǽst jiər]

きらい【嫌い】 **hate** [heit]

→ 私は虫が嫌いです。 *I hate bugs.*

キリン **giraffe** [dʒərǽf]

きる【切る】 **cut** [kʌt]　過去形 cut [kʌt]（同形）

【着る】 **put on** [put ɑn]（シャツなどを）過去形 put [put]（同形）

→ ケーキをナイフで6個に分けてください。 *Please cut the cake into six pieces with a knife.*

→ パジャマを着なさい。 *Put on your pajamas.*

◉ くつをはく＝put on shoes

きれいにする **clean** [kliːn] ＝そうじする

→ テーブルの上をきれいにしてください。

*Please clean the table.*

きれいな **clean** [kliːn] ⇔ dirty ＝せいけつな

→ きれいなハンカチを持ってますか? *Do you have a clean handkerchief?*

きろく(する)【〜を記録(する)】 **record** [rikɔ́ːrd]

◉「きろく」という名詞ではアクセントが前にくることもあります。

きをつける【気をつける】 **take care** [teik keər]
**watch out** [wɑtʃ aut]

きんいろ【金色】 **gold** [gould]

きんこ【金庫】 **safe** [seif] ＝あんぜんな

ぎんこう【銀行】 **bank** [bæŋk]

→ ぼくはあの銀行に10万円貯金しました。 *I put one hundred thousand yen in that bank.*

きんようび【金曜日】 **Friday** [fráidei]

→ 私は金曜日にピアノの練習をします。 *I practice the piano on Friday.*

# く ク

くうき【空気】 **air** [eər] ＝そら

くうこう【空港】 **airport** [éərpɔːrt]

くがつ【9月】 **September** [septémbər]

→ カナダでは, 9月から新学期です。 *In Canada, the school year starts in September.*

くさ【草】 **grass** [græs]

くしゃみ(をする) **sneeze** [sniːz] ◉ ハクション＝Ahchoo

クジラ **whale** [ʰweil]

ください **give** [giv] 過去形 gave [geiv] ＝くれる, あげ
**have** [hæv] 過去形 had [hæd, həd]

→ 水をください。 *Please give me a glass of water*

→ ハンバーガーをください。（店などで注文する時）

*Can I have a hamburger, please?*

くだもの【果物】 **fruit** [fruːt]

くち【口】 **mouth** [mauθ]

→ 口の中に物が入ったまま話してはいけません。

*Do not speak with your mouth full.*

くつ【靴】 **shoe(s)** [ʃuː(z)]

クッキー **cookie** [kúki]

→ 誰がクッキーをぬすんだの? *Who stole the cookies?*

くっつける **glue** [gluː]

en
ja
ja

ja

ja

ja
ja
ja
ja
ja
ja

ja

ja

ja

ja

ja

ja

ja

ja

ja

ja

ja

ja

ja

ja

ja

ja

ja

ja

ja

ja

ja

ja

ja

ja

ja

ja

ja

ja

ja

ja

ja
# く

→ この部分と, この部分をくっつけなさい。 *Glue this part and this part together.*

くつした【靴下】 **sock(s)** [sɑk(s)]

くつや【靴屋】 **shoe store** [ʃúː stɔːr]

くばる【配る】 **hand (...out)** [hænd] ＝わたす, て

→ これをみんなにくばってください。 *Hand these out to everyone.*

くび【首】 **neck** [nck]

クマ **bear** [beər]

くも【雲】 **cloud** [klaud]

クモ **spider** [spáidər]

くもりの【曇りの】 **cloudy** [kláudi]

くらい【暗い】 **dark** [dɑːrk] ⇔ light あかるい

→ 暗くなってきました。 *It is getting dark.*

クラス **class** [klæs] ＝じゅぎょう

クラブ **club** [klʌb]

→ ぼくは野球部です。 *I'm a member of the baseball club.* ● クラブ活動＝club activities

くりかえす【繰り返す】 **repeat** [ripíːt]

→ 私の言うことを繰り返してください。 *Please repeat after me.*

クリックする **click** [klik]

くる【来る】 **come** [kʌm] 過去形 came [keim]

→ ここに来なさい。 *Come here.*

→ 早くいらっしゃい! 今,行ってるところだよ。 *Are you coming? I'm coming!*

グループ **group** [gruːp]

くるま【車】 **car** [kɑːr] ＝じどうしゃ

→ 車に乗って。 *Get in the car.*

くるまいす【車いす】 **wheelchair** [wíːltʃèər]

グレー **gray** [grei]

グレープフルーツ **grapefruit** [gréipfruːt]

くれる **give** [giv] 過去形 gave [geiv] ＝ください, あたえる

→ 父はぼくにいい辞書をくれた。 *My father gave me a nice dictionary.*

くろ【黒】 **black** [blæk]

# け ケ

けいかく(する)【計画(する)】 **plan** [plæn] ＝よてい

● ～を計画している＝I am planning to...

けいこ(する) **lesson** [lesn] ＝じゅぎょう
**practice** [præktis] ＝れんしゅうする

けいさつかん【警察官】 **police officer** [pəlíːs ɔ̀fisər]

けいたいでんわ【携帯電話】 **cellular phone** [séljulər fòun]

ケーキ **cake** [keik]

→ ケーキの大きいのをもらっていいですか? *May I have the big piece (of cake)?*

けがをする【怪我をする】 **hurt** [həːrt] ＝きずつく

けしゴム【消しゴム】 **eraser** [iréisər] ＝こくばんふき

→ 消しゴムを借りてもいいですか? *Can I use your eraser?*

けす【消す】 **turn off** [təːrn ɔ(ː)f]
【消す】 **erase** [iréis] (消しゴムや黒板ふきで消す)

● 明かりを消す＝turn off the light

けちな **stingy** [stíndʒi]

→ けちけちしないで。 *Don't be stingy.*

けっこんする【結婚する】 **marry** [mæri]

けっして【決して～でない】 **never** [névər]

けっせきの【欠席の】 **absent** [æbsənt] ＝やすんで

→ 今日はこうじくんが欠席です。 *Koji is absent from school today.*

げつようび【月曜日】 **Monday** [mʌ́ndei]

→ ぼくは月曜日に野球をします。 *I play baseball on Monday.*

けむし【毛虫】 **caterpillar** [kǽtərpilər] ＝イモムシ

けむり【煙】 **smoke** [smouk] ＝タバコをすう

ける【蹴る】 **kick** [kik]

けんか **fight** [fait] ＝たたかう

→ 昨日弟とけんかした。 *I had a fight with my little brother yesterday.*

→ けんかはやめて! *Stop fighting!*

げんきな【元気な】 **fine** [fain], **healthy** [hélθi] (健康な)

げんご【言語】 **language** [lǽŋgwidʒ] ＝ことば

# こ コ

コイン **coin** [kɔin] ＝こうか

こうえん【公園】 **park** [pɑːrk] (木のある公園)
**playground** [pléigràund] (遊具のある公園)

こうか【硬貨】 **coin** [kɔin] ＝コイン

ja
ja

ja
ja
ja
ja
ja
ja
ja

ja

ja

ja

ja

ja

ja

ja

ja

ja

ja

ja

ja

ja

ja

ja

ja

ja

ja

ja

ja

ja

ja

ja

ja

ja

ja

ja

ja

ja

ja

ja

ja

ja

ja

ja

ja

ja

ja

ja

ja

ja

ja
ja
ja
ja
ja

ja

ja

ja

ja

ja

ja

ja
ja
ja

ja

ja

ja
ja
ja
ja
ja
ja

ja

ja
ja
ja

ja
ja
ja

ja
ja
ja
ja
ja

ja

ja

ja

ja

ja

ja

ja

ja

ja

ja

ja

ja

ja

ja

ja

ja

ja

ja

ja

ja

ja

ja

ja

ja

ja

ja

ja

ja
ja

ja

ja

ja

ja

ja

ja
ja
ja

ja

ja
ja

ja

ja
ja
ja
ja

ja

ja

ja
ja
ja

ja

ja

ja

ja

ja

ja

ja

ja

ja

ja

ja

ja

ja

ja

ja

ja

ja

ja

ja

ja

ja

ja

ja

ja

ja

ja

ja

ja

ja

ja

ja

ja

ja

ja

ja

ja

ja

ja

ja

ja

ja

ja

ja

ja

ja

ja

ja

ja

ja

ja

ja

ja

ja

ja

ja

ja

ja

ja

ja

ja

ja

ja

ja

ja

ja

ja

ja

ja

ja

ja

ja

ja

ja

ja

ja
ja

ja

ja

ja

ja

ja

ja
ja
ja

ja

ja

ja
ja
ja
ja
ja
ja

ja

ja
ja
ja

ja
ja
ja

ja
ja
ja
ja
ja
ja
ja

ja
ja
ja
ja
ja
ja

ja

ja

ja

ja

ja

ja

ja

ja

ja

ja

ja

ja

ja

ja

ja

ja

ja

ja

ja

ja

ja

ja

ja

ja

ja

ja

ja
ja

ja

ja

ja

ja

ja

ja
ja
ja

ja

ja
ja

ja

ja
ja
ja
ja

ja

ja

ja
ja
ja

ja
ja
ja

ja
ja
ja
ja
ja
ja
ja

ja

ja

ja

ja

ja

ja

ja

ja

ja

ja

ja

ja

ja

ja

ja

ja

ja

ja

ja

ja

ja

ja

ja

ja

ja

ja
ja

ja

ja

ja

ja

ja

ja
ja
ja

ja

ja
ja

ja

ja
ja
ja
ja

ja

ja

ja
ja
ja

ja
ja
ja

ja
ja
ja
ja
ja
ja
ja

ja
ja
ja
ja
ja
ja

ja

ja

ja

ja

ja

ja

ja

ja

ja

ja

ja

ja

ja

ja

ja

ja

ja

ja

ja

ja

ja

ja

ja

ja

ja

ja

ja

ja

ja

ja

ja

ja

ja

ja

ja

ja

ja

ja

ja

ja

ja

ja

ja

ja

ja

ja

ja

ja

ja

ja

ja

ja

ja

ja

ja

ja

ja

ja

ja

ja

ja

ja

ja

ja

ja

ja

ja

ja

ja

ja

ja

ja

ja

ja

ja

ja

ja

ja

ja

ja

ja

ja
ja

ja

ja

ja

ja

ja

ja
ja
ja

ja

ja
ja

ja

ja
ja
ja
ja

ja

ja

ja
ja
ja

ja
ja
ja

ja
ja
ja
ja
ja
ja
ja

ja
ja
ja
ja
ja
ja

ja

ja

ja

ja

ja

ja

ja

ja

ja

ja

ja

ja

ja

ja

ja

ja

ja

ja

ja

ja

ja

ja

ja

ja

ja

ja

ja

ja

ja

ja

ja

ja

ja

ja

ja

ja

ja

ja

ja

ja

ja

ja

ja

ja

ja

ja

ja

ja

ja

ja

ja

ja

ja

ja

ja

ja

ja

ja

ja

ja

ja

ja

ja

ja

ja

ja

ja

ja

ja

ja

ja

ja

ja

ja

ja

ja

ja

ja

ja

ja
ja

ja

ja

ja

ja

ja

ja
ja
ja

ja

ja
ja

ja

ja
ja
ja
ja

ja

ja

ja
ja
ja

ja
ja
ja

ja
ja
ja
ja
ja
ja
ja

ja
ja
ja
ja
ja
ja

ja

ja

ja

ja

ja

ja

ja

ja

ja

ja

ja

ja

ja

ja

ja

ja

ja

ja

ja

ja

ja

ja

ja

ja

ja

ja

ja

ja

ja

ja

ja

ja

ja

ja

ja

ja

ja

ja

ja

ja

ja

ja

ja

ja

ja

ja

ja

ja

ja

ja

ja

ja

ja

ja

ja

ja

ja

ja

ja

ja

ja

ja

ja

ja

ja

ja

ja

ja

ja

ja

ja

ja

ja

ja

ja

ja

ja

ja

ja

ja

ja

ja

ja

ja

ja

ja

ja

ja

ja

ja

ja

ja

ja

ja

こうこう【高校】(senior [síːniər]) high school
　● 中学校 = junior[dʒúːnjər] high school

こうさく【工作】handicrafts [hændikrəft]

こうさする【交差する】cross [krɔːs] = わたる

こうちゃ【紅茶】tea [tiː]
　● アイスティーは iced[aist] tea と言います。

こうちょうせんせい【校長先生】principal [prínsəpəl]

こうふんした【興奮した】excited [iksáitid]

コウモリ　bat [bæt]

こえ【声】voice [vɔis]

コーヒー　coffee [kɔ́ːfi]

コーラ　cola [kóulə]

ごがつ【5月】May [mei]

こくご【国語】Japanese [dʒæpaníːz] = にほんご

こくさいてきな【国際的な】international [intərnǽʃənəl]

こくばん【黒板】blackboard [blǽkbɔːrd]
　➡ 黒板に答えを書きなさい。　Write the answer on the blackboard.

こくばんふき【黒板ふき】eraser [iréisər] = けしごむ

ココア　hot chocolate [hát tʃɔ́ːkəlit]
　● cocoa [kóukou] とも言います。

ここに　here [hiər] = さあ, はい
　➡ ここに来なさい。　Come here.

コショウ　pepper [pépər]
　➡ コショウを取ってください。　Pass me the pepper, please.

こたえる【答える】answer [ǽnsər] = へんじ

こちら　this [ðis] = これ, この　複数形 these [ðiːz]
　➡ こちらは私の英語の先生です。　This is my English teacher.

コック　cook [kuk] = りょうりする
　➡ 彼は有名なホテルでコックとして働いています。　He works as a cook at a famous hotel.

こっけいな　funny [fʌ́ni] = おかしな, おもしろい

コップ　glass [glæs]

こていする【固定する】fix [fiks] = なおす

こと【事】thing [θiŋ] = もの

～ごと　every [évri] = まい～
　➡ 10分ごとに電車が来ます。　The train runs every ten minutes.

～ことがある　sometimes [sʌ́mtàims]

ことし【今年】this year [ðis jiər]

ことば【言葉】language [lǽŋgwidʒ] = げんご
　● 話し言葉 = spoken[spóukən] language
　● 書き言葉 = written[rítən] language

こども【子供】child [tʃaild]　複数形 children [tʃíldrən]　kid [kid]

この　this [ðis] = こちら, これ
　➡ このかばんは私のものです。　This bag is mine.
　● 2つ以上の物をさす時は these [ðiːz]

ごはん【ご飯】meal[miːl], rice[rais]
　● 炊いたごはん = steamed rice [stíːmd rais]
　● 調理したごはん = cooked rice [kúkt rais]
　● やきめし = fried rice [fraid rais]

ごめんなさい　sorry [sɔ́ri] = ざんねんな
　➡ 遅れてごめんなさい。　I'm sorry I'm late.

ゴルフ　golf [gɑlf]

これ　this [ðis] = この, こちら　複数形 these [ðiːz]

これら　these [ðiːz]　this の複数形
　➡ これ(ら)は私の鉛筆です。　These are my pencils.

ころす【殺す】kill [kil]

ころぶ【転ぶ】fall [fɔːl] = おちる　過去形 fell [fel]
　➡ 床はすべりやすいので気をつけて。転ばないように。　The floor is slippery. Be careful. Don't fall down.

こわい【怖い】scary [skéəri]

こわがって　afraid [əfréid]
　➡ 私は犬がこわい。　I am afraid of dogs.
　● ～をこわがる = be afraid of...

こわす【壊す】break[breik] = やぶる　過去形 broke [brouk]

こわれた【壊れた】be broken [bróukən]
　➡ ぼくのテレビゲームが壊れた。　My video game is broken.

こんにちは　hello [helóu] = もしもし

こんばん【今晩】tonight [tənáit]　this evening [ðis íːvniŋ]
　➡ こんばんは。　Good evening.

こんちゅう【昆虫】bug [bʌg] = むし

コンピューター　computer [kəmpjúːtər]
　➡ あなたはコンピューターを使えますか?　Can you use a computer?

こんろ　stove [stouv]

## さ サ

さあ　**here** [híər]　＝ここに, はい
➡ さあどうぞ。　*Here you are.*

さいごの【最後の】 **last** [lǽst]　⇔ first
➡ 1年の最後の月は12月です。　*The last month of the year is December.*

さいじつ【祭日】 **holiday** [hálidèi]　＝きゅうじつ

さいしょの【最初の】 **first** [fə́ːrst]　⇔ last
➡ 1年の最初の月は1月です。　*The first month of the year is January.*

サイズ　**size** [saiz]

さいふ【財布】 **wallet** [wálit]

さかさまの【逆さまの】 **upside down** [ʌ́psaid daun]
➡ 写真が逆さまです。　*The picture is upside down.*

さがす【(〜)を探す】 **look for...** [luk fər]
➡ 私のかばんを探しています。　*I am looking for my bag.*

さかな【魚】 **fish** [fiʃ]　複数形 **fish** [fiʃ]（単複同形）
● イカ＝squid [skwid], エビ＝shrimp [ʃrimp], サケ＝salmon [sǽmən], サメ＝shark [ʃɑːrk], タイ＝sea bream [briːm], タコ＝octopus [áktəpəs], ヒラメ＝flounder [fláundər], マグロ＝tuna [túːna]

さけぶ【叫ぶ】 **cry** [krai]　＝なく
　　　　　　**shout** [ʃaut]

サッカー　**soccer** [sákər]

サッカーせんしゅ【サッカー選手】 **soccer player** [pléiər]
➡ ぼくは大きくなったらサッカー選手になりたい。
*I want to be a soccer player when I grow up.*

ざっし【雑誌】 **magazine** [mægəzíːn]

さっそく　**at once** [ət wʌ́ns]　＝すぐに

さとう【砂糖】 **sugar** [ʃúgər]

さなぎ　**pupa** [pjúːpə]

〜さま【〜様(手紙の書き出しで)】 **Dear** [diər] ＝しんあいなる

さむい【寒い】 **cold** [kould]　⇔ hot

さようなら　**goodbye** [gúdbài]

さら【皿】 **plate** [pleit]

サラダ　**salad** [sǽləd]

さる【去る】 **leave** [liːv] ＝しゅっぱつする, わすれる, しておく

サル　**monkey** [mʌ́ŋki]

さわがしい【騒がしい】 **noisy** [nɔ́izi]　⇔ quiet

さわぐ【騒ぐ】 **make noise** [meik nɔiz]

さわる【触る】 **touch** [tʌtʃ]　＝ふれる

〜さん　**Mr.** [místər]（男性の場合） ＝〜し, 〜せんせい
　　　　**Ms.** [miz]（女性の場合 ※結婚・未婚に関係なく）
　　　　**Mrs.** [mísiz]（結婚している女性の場合）
　　　　**Miss** [mis]（未婚の女性の場合）

さんかする【参加する】 **take part in** [teik pɑːrt in]
➡ ぼくは昨日運動会に参加した。　*I took part in sports day at school yesterday.*

さんがつ【3月】 **March** [mɑːrtʃ]

さんすう【算数】 **math** [mæθ]

さんせいする【賛成する】 **agree** [əgríː]
➡ 私はあなたに賛成します。　*I agree with you.*

サンタクロース　**Santa Claus** [sǽntə klɔ́ːz]

サンドイッチ　**sandwich** [sǽnwitʃ]

ざんねんな【残念な】 **sorry** [sɔ́ːri]　＝ごめんなさい
➡ それは残念ですね。　*I'm sorry to hear that.*

さんぽする【散歩する】 **take a walk** [teik ə wɔːk]
過去形 **took a walk** [tuk ə wɔːk]
➡ ぼくは今朝お父さんと長い間散歩しました。　*I took a long walk with my father this morning.*

## し シ

し【死】 **death** [deθ]

〜し【氏】 **Mr.** [místər]　＝〜さん, 〜せんせい

じ【〜時】 **o'clock** [əklák]
➡ もう7時だ。　*It's almost seven o'clock.*

しあい【試合】 **game** [geim]
● 野球の試合＝baseball game

シーソー　**seesaw** [síːsɔː]

ジーパン　**jeans** [dʒíːnz]

ジェットき【ジェット機】 **jet** [jet]

しお【塩】 **salt** [sɔːlt]

しがつ【4月】 **April** [éiprəl]

しかる　**scold** [skould]
➡ 先生に叱られた。　*I was scolded by my teacher.*

じかん【時間】 **hour** [áuər]（時間の単位）
　　　　【時間】 **time** [taim]（時刻）

➡ 1日は24時間です。 *There are 24 hours in a day.*

➡ いつも何時に寝ますか? *What time do you usually go to bed?*

**じかんわり** **class schedule** [skédʒuːl]

◉ 列車の時刻表は timetable [táimtèibl] と言います。

**しき**【式】 **ceremony** [sérəmouni]

◉ 始業式 = opening ceremony [óupəniŋ]

◉ 終業式 = closing ceremony [klóuziŋ]

**しけん**【試験】 **examination** [igzæmənéiʃən]

**じこ**【事故】 **accident** [æksidənt]

**しごと**【仕事】 **job** [dʒɑb] = しょくぎょう

【仕事】 **occupation** [àkjəpéiʃən] = しょくぎょう

【仕事】 **work** [wəːrk] = はたらく, べんきょうする

**じしょ**【辞書】 **dictionary** [díkʃəneri]

➡ 辞書を借りてもいいですか? *May I use your dictionary?*

**じしん**【地震】 **earthquake** [ə́ːrθkwèik]

**しずかな** **quiet** [kwáiət] (音のない) ⇔ noisy さわがしい

**silent** [sáilənt] = だまった

**しずかにする**【静かにする】 **be quiet** [kwáiət]

➡ 静かにしなさい。 *Be quiet.*

**しずく** **drop** [drɑp] = おちる

**しぜん**【自然】 **nature** [néitʃər]

**～しそこなう** **miss** [mis] = (～が)いなくてさびしい

**～した** **did** [did] do の過去形 didn't ～しなかった

**したに**【(～の)下に】 **under** [ʌ́ndər]

➡ あなたの猫はいすの下にいるよ。 *Your cat is under the chair.*

**したい** **want to...** [wɑ́nt tə]

➡ 英語を上手に話したいです。 *I want to speak English well.*

**したしくなる**【親しくなる】 **make friends with...**

[méik fréndz wið] 過去形 made [meid] friends with

**しちがつ**【7月】 **July** [dʒulái]

**じつぎょうか**【実業家】 **businessman** [bíznismæn]

**じっている**【知っている】 **know** [nou] 過去形 knew [njuː]

➡ 私はコンピューターの使い方を知っています。 *I know how to use a computer.*

**しっぱいする**【失敗する】 **fail** [feil]

➡ 試験に失敗した。 *I failed my exam.*

**しつもん**【質問】 **question** [kwéstʃən] = もんだい

➡ 何か質問はありますか? *Do you have any questions?*

**しつれいな**【失礼な】 **rude** [ruːd]

**しつれいですが～**【失礼ですが】 **Excuse me, ...** [ikskjúːz miː]

**していただけますか** **Would you...?** [wud júː]

(何かをていねいに依頼する表現)

**しておく**【(～の状態に)しておく】 **leave** [liːv] 過去形 left [left] = さる, しゅっぱつする, わすれる

➡ ドアをあけっぱなしにしないでください。 *Don't leave the door open.*

**～してくれませんか** **Will you...?** [wil júː] (何かをたのむ表現) = ～しませんか

➡ コーヒーをもう1杯もらっていいですか? *Will you give me another cup of coffee?*

**してはいけない** **mustn't** [mʌ́sənt] = must not

➡ お母さんにうそをついてはいけません。 *You mustn't lie to your mother.*

**してもよい** **may** [mei] (許可を表す) = かもしれない

➡ 中に入ってもよいですか? *May I come in?*

**じてんしゃ**【自転車】 **bicycle** [báisikl] = bike [baik]

**じどうしゃ**【自動車】 **car** [kɑːr] = くるま

**しない** **not** [nɑt] = ～でない ※助動詞や動詞の後ろに付いて「～ではない」(否定)を表す

**しなければならない** **have to...** [hæv tə], **must** [mʌst]

➡ 今夜は塾に行かなくてはいけません。 *I have to go to juku tonight.*

➡ もう行かなくては。 *I have to go now.*

**しぬ**【死ぬ】 **die** [dai]

**しはらう**【支払う】 **pay** [pei] 過去形 paid [peid]

➡ このシャツにいくら払った? *How much did you pay for this shirt?*

**しま**【島】 **island** [áilənd]

**シマウマ** **zebra** [zíːbrə]

**～しませんか** **Will you...?** [wil júː] (誘う表現)

➡ いっしょに…しませんか? *Will you join us?*

**じむいん**【事務員】 **office clerk** [ɔ́ːfis kləːrk]

**しめる**【閉める】 **close** [klouz], **shut** [ʃʌt] 過去形 shu

➡ 窓を閉めてください。 *Please close the window*

**シャープペンシル** **mechanical pencil** [məkǽnikəl pénsəl]

しゃかいか【社会科】 **social studies** [sóuʃəl stʌ̀diəz]

ジャガイモ **potato** [pətéitou]

しやくしょ【市役所】 **city hall** [síti hɔ̀:l]

しゃしん【写真】 **photo** [fóutòu], **picture** [píktʃər] ＝え

シャツ **shirt** [ʃə:rt]

ジャックオーランタン **jack-o' lantern** [dʒǽkələ̀ntərn]
 （＝かぼちゃのちょうちん）
 ➡ かぼちゃのちょうちんを（彫って）作ろうよ。
  *Let's carve a jack-o'-lantern.*

しゃべる **talk** [tɔ:k] ＝はなす

シャボンだま **bubble** [bʌbl] ＝あわ

ジャングルジム **jungle gym** [dʒʌ́ŋgl dʒìm]

ジャンプする **jump** [dʒʌmp] ＝とぶ

しゅう【週】 **week** [wi:k] ◉ 今週＝this week
 ◉ 来週＝next week  ◉ 先週＝last week

じゅういちがつ【11月】 **November** [nouvémbər]

じゅうがつ【10月】 **October** [ɑktóubər]

じゅうしょ【住所】 **address** [ədrés, ǽdres] ＝あてさき

ジュース **juice** [dʒu:s]

じゆうな【自由な】 **free** [fri:] ＝ひまな, むりょうの, ただの

じゅうにがつ【12月】 **December** [disémbər]
 ➡ 12月は1年の12番目の月です。*December is the*
  *twelfth month of the year.*

じゅうぶんな【十分な】 **enough** [inʌf]

しゅうまつ【週末】 **weekend** [wí:kənd]
 ◉ この週末＝this weekend

じゅうような【重要な】 **important** [impɔ́:rtənt]
 ＝たいせつな

じゅぎょう【授業】 **class** [klæs] ＝クラス
     **lesson** [lesn] ＝けいこ

しゅくだいをする【宿題をする】 **do (one's) homework**
 [hóumwə̀rk] 過去形 **did (one's) homework**
 ➡ 夕食の前に宿題をしなさい。*Do your homework*
  *before dinner.*

しゅっしん【～出身（である）】 **be from...** [bi: frɑm]
 ➡ 私は福岡出身です。*I am from Fukuoka.*

しゅっぱつする【出発する】 **leave** [li:v] ＝さる, しておく
     **start** [stɑ:rt] ＝はじまる, はじめる
 ◉ ～へ向かって出発する＝leave for...
 ➡ 私は毎朝8時に家を出ます（学校に向かいます）。
  *I leave for school at eight o'clock every*
  *morning.*

しゅと【首都】 **capital** [kǽpitl]

しゅみ【趣味】 **hobby** [hɑbi]

じゅんびする【準備する】 **prepare** [pripéər] ＝よういする
    【準備できて】 **ready** [rédi]
 ➡ 準備ができてるよ。*I'm ready.*

～しよう **Let's...** [lets]

しょうかいする【紹介する】 **introduce** [ìntrədjú:s]

しょうがっこう【小学校】 **elementary school**
 [èləméntəri sku:l]
 ➡ ぼくは浜寺小学校に通っています。*I go to*
  *Hamadera Elementary School.*

じょうぎ【定規】 **ruler** [rú:lər]
 ➡ 定規で線を引きなさい。*Draw a line with a ruler.*

しょうご【正午】 **noon** [nu:n]

しょうじきな【正直な】 **honest** [ɑ́nist]

じょうしき【常識】 **common sense** [kɑ́mən sens]

じょうずに【上手に】 **well** [wel]
 ➡ 私は英語をじょうずに読めます。*I can read*
  *English well.*

しょうたいする【招待する】 **invite** [inváit] ＝よぶ

じょうだん【冗談】 **joke** [jouk]
 ◉ 冗談を言う＝make a joke

～しようとする **try** [trai] ＝ためす

しょうぼうし【消防士】 **firefighter** [fáiərfàitər]

しょうぼうしょ【消防署】 **fire station** [fáiər stèiʃən]

しょうめん【（～の）正面に】 **in front of** [in frʌnt əv]
 ➡ 学校の正面に大きな図書館があります。*There is*
  *a big library in front of our school.*

しょうらい【将来】 **future** [fjú:tʃər] ＝みらい

ジョギング **jogging** [dʒɑ́giŋ]

しょくぎょう【職業】 **job** [dʒɑb] ＝しごと
   【職業】 **occupation** [ɑ̀kjəpéiʃən] ＝しごと

しょくじ【食事】 **meal** [mi:l] ＝ごはん

しょくたく【食卓】 **table** [teibl]
 ◉ 食卓の準備をする＝set the table

しょくどう【食堂】 **dining room** [dáiniŋ rù:m]

しょくぶつ【植物】 **plant** [plænt]

じょし【女子】 **girl** [gə:rl]

しょっちゅう **often** [ɔ́(:)fən] ＝よく, たびたび

しろ【白】 **white** [hwait]

しんあいなる【親愛なる】 **Dear** [diər]

= ～さま（手紙の書き出しで）

しんかんせん【新幹線】 **bullet train** [búlit trèin]

しんごう【信号】 **traffic light** [træfik lait]

しんしつ【寝室】 **bedroom** [bédru:m]

しんじる【信じる】 **believe** [bilí:v]

しんせき【親戚】 **relative** [rélətiv]

しんせつな【親切な】 **kind** [kaind] ＝やさしい

　➡ 妹に親切にしなさい。 *Be kind to your little sister.*

しんぞう【心臓】 **heart** [hɑːrt]

しんだ【死んだ】 **dead** [ded]

しんぱいする【心配する】 **worry** [wə́ːri]

　➡ あなたのことが心配です。心配しないで。
　*I'm worried about you.  Don't worry.*

しんぶん【新聞】 **newspaper** [njú:zpèipər]

しんや【深夜】 **midnight** [mídnait]

# す　ス

す【巣】 **nest** [nest]

すいえい【水泳】 **swimming** [swímiŋ]

スイカ **watermelon** [wɔ́:tərmèlən]

すいぞくかん【水族館】 **aquarium** [əkwéːriəm]

すいそくする【推測する】 **guess** [ges] ＝おもう, いいあてる

すいはんき【炊飯器】 **rice cooker** [ráis kùkər]

すいようび【水曜日】 **Wednesday** [wénzdei]

スーパーマーケット **supermarket** [sú:pərmà:rkit]

スープ **soup** [su:p]

スカート **skirt** [skəːrt]

すき【好き】 **like** [laik], **love** [lʌv] ＝あいしている

　➡ 私はりんごが好きです。 *I like apples.*

　➡ これはどうですか? *How do you like it?*

　➡ 私は音楽が大好きです。 *I love music.*

すきな【好きな】 **favorite** [féivərit]

　➡ 君の好きな果物は? *What is your favorite fruit?*

スキー **skiing** [skí:iŋ]

スキーをする **ski** [ski:]

　➡ 私はスキーができます。 *I can ski.*

スキップをする **skip** [skip]

すくなくとも【少なくとも】 **at least** [ət lí:st]

すぐに **right away** [ráit əwèi], **right now** [nau],

**at once** [ət wʌ́ns] ＝さっそく

　➡ 今すぐにやりなさい。 *Do it right now.*

スケート **skating** [skéitiŋ]

スケートをする **skate** [skeit]

スケートボード **skateboarding** [skéitbɔ̀:rdiŋ]

ずこう【図工】 **arts and crafts** [á:rts ənd kræfs]

すこししかない【少ししかない】 **few** [fju:], **little** [litl]

　➡ 冬にはほとんど雪がふりません。 *We have little snow in the winter.*

すこしは【少しは】 **a little** [ə lítl]

　➡ 私は英語が少し話せます。 *I can speak English a little.*

すこしも～ない **not ...any**, **not ... at all**

　➡ もう1枚もクッキーは残っていません。 *There are not any cookies left.*

すず【鈴】 **bell** [bel] ＝ベル, かね

すずしい【涼しい】 **cool** [ku:l]

すすめる【勧める】 **advise** [ədváis]

スチュワーデス **flight attendant** [flait əténdənt]

ずつう【頭痛】 **headache** [hédèik]

ステーキ **steak** [steik]

すてきな【素敵な】 **nice** [nais], **good** [gud]

すな【砂】 **sand** [sænd]

スパゲティ **spaghetti** [spəgéti]

スプーン **spoon** [spu:n]

～すべき **should** [ʃud] ＝～べきである

すべて【全て】 **everything** [évriθiŋ] ＝ぜんぶ

すべて(の)【全て(の)】 **all** [ɔ:l], **every** [évri]

すべりだい【滑り台】 **slide** [slaid]

スポーツ **sport** [spɔ:rt]

ズボン **pants** [pænts]

すもうとり **sumo wrestler** [réslər] ＝りきし

スリッパ **slipper** [slípər] (通常はsを付けて slippers)

する **do** [du:], **does** [dʌs, dəz] 過去形 **did** [did]

　➡ 何をしているの? *What are you doing?*

する【(チーム戦のスポーツを)する】 **play** [plei]

　＝あそぶ,(楽器などを)ひく

　➡ 放課後サッカーをしようよ。 *Let's play soccer after school.*

すわる【座る】 **sit** [sit] 過去形 **sat** [sæt]

すんでいる【住んでいる】 **live** [liv]

→ 私は東京に住んでいます。　*I live in Tokyo.*

# せ　セ

せいかつ【生活】**life** [laif]　＝いのち

せいき【世紀】**century** [séntʃəri]

● 21世紀 = the 21th century

せいけつな【清潔な】**clean** [kli:n] ⇔ dirty よごれた

せいこうする【成功する】**succeed** [səksí:d]

せいじか【政治家】**politician** [pàlitíʃən]

せいせき【成績】**grade** [greid]　＝がくねん

【成績】**score** [skɔ:r]　＝とくてん

せいちょうする【成長する】**grow** [grou]　＝そだてる

せいと【生徒】**student** [stjú:dənt]　＝がくせい

せいりょういんりょうすい【清涼飲料水】**soft drink**

[sɔ́ft driŋk]

セーター　**sweater** [swétər]

せかい【世界】**world** [wə:rld]

● 世界中 = all over the world

せき【席】**seat** [si:t]

→ 席についてください。　*Please be seated.*

→ この席は空いていますか（だれかがすわりますか）？

*Is this seat taken?*

せっけん【石けん】**soap** [soup]

ぜったい〜ない【絶対〜ない】**never** [névər]

セットする　**set** [set]　＝おく　過去形 **set** [set]（同形）

● 位置について, ヨーイ, ドン! = Ready, set, go!

せつめいする【（〜を）説明する】**explain** [ikspléin]

せなか【背中】**back** [bæk]　＝うしろ（の）

せわをする【（〜の）世話をする】**take care of...**

[téik kèər əv]　過去形 **took care of** [túk kèər əv]

→ 私は自分の犬の世話をしなければいけません。

*I have to take care of my dog.*

せんげつ【先月】**last month** [lǽst mʌnθ]

せんじつ【先日】**the other day** [ði ʌ́ðər dei]

せんしゅ【選手】**player** [pléiər]

せんしゅう【先週】**last week** [lǽst wi:k]

せんせい【先生】**teacher** [tí:tʃər],

（男の先生の場合）**Mr.** [místər]

● 女の先生の場合 = Ms. [miz], 女性で結婚している先生

= Mrs. [mísiz], 女性で未婚の先生 = Miss [mis]

ぜんぜん〜ない　**not ...at all**　＝すこしも〜ない

→ 私は全然スキーができない。　*I cannot ski at all.*

せんそう【戦争】**war** [wɔ:r]

ぜんぶ【全部】**everything** [évriθìŋ], **all** [ɔ:l]

# そ　ソ

ゾウ　**elephant** [éləfənt]

そうじ【掃除】**cleaning** [klí:niŋ]

そうじき【そうじ機】**vacuum cleaner** [vǽkjuəm klì:nər]

→ 自分の部屋にそうじ機をかけて。　*Vacuum your room.*

そうじする　**clean** [kli:n]　＝きれいにする

→ トイレをそうじしなさい。　*Clean the toilet.*

そくたつ【速達】**express** [iksprés]　＝きゅうこう

そこ【底】**bottom** [bátəm]

そこに　**there** [ðeər]　＝〜がある

そだてる【育てる】**grow** [grou]　＝せいちょうする

過去形 **grew** [gru:]

そつぎょう【卒業】**graduation** [grædʒuéiʃən]

● 卒業式 = graduation ceremony [sérəmóuni]

● 卒業生 = graduate [grǽdʒuèit]

そっと　**quietly** [kwáiətli]

そとへ【（〜の）外へ】**outside** [áutsàid]

そのうち　**soon** [su:n]

そのとき【その時】**then** [ðen]　＝それから, それでは

そばに　**by** [bai], **near** [niər]

→ 私のそばにすわって。　*Sit by me.*

そふ【祖父】**grandfather** [grǽnfà:ðər]　＝おじいさん

● おじいちゃん = grandpa [grǽnpɑ:]

ソファ　**sofa** [sóufə]

そぼ【祖母】**grandmother** [grǽnmʌ̀ðər]　＝おばあさん

● おばあちゃん = grandma [grǽnmɑ:]

そら【空】**sky** [skai], **air** [eər]　＝くうき

そよかぜ　**breeze** [bri:z]

それから　**then** [ðen]　＝そのとき

それぞれ（の）　**each** [i:tʃ]

それでは　**then** [ðen]　＝それから

それは（が, を, に）　**it** [it]

→ それは私のふでばこです。　*It's my pencil case.*

そんけいする【尊敬する】**respect** [rìspékt]

→ 他人を尊重しなさい。　*Respect others.*

# た タ

たいいく〖体育〗 **P.E.** [pːiː]
　= Physical Education [fízikəl édʒkéiʃən]

たいいくかん〖体育館〗 **gym** [dʒim]

だいがく〖大学〗 **university** [jùːnivə́ːrsəti]
　　　　　　 **college** [kálidʒ]

たいくつな〖退屈な〗 **boring** [bɔ́ːriŋ]
　➡ この本はおもしろくない。私は退屈です。 *This book is boring. I'm bored.*

たいざいする〖滞在する〗 **stay** [stei]
　◉ ～に滞在する = stay at...

だいじょうぶ〖大丈夫〗 **all right** [ɔ́ːl rait]　= へいき
　➡ 大丈夫ですか？ *Are you all right?*

たいせつな〖大切な〗 **important** [impɔ́ːrtənt]
　= じゅうような
　➡ 英語を勉強するのは大切です。 *It's important to study English.*

だいとうりょう〖大統領〗 **the president** [prézidənt]

だいどころ〖台所〗 **kitchen** [kítʃin]

たいよう〖太陽〗 **sun** [sʌn]　= ひ

たいよう〖大洋〗 **ocean** [óuʃən]　= うみ

タオル **towel** [táuəl]

たかい〖(値段が)高い〗 **expensive** [ikspénsiv] ⇔cheap
　〖(人や木が)高い〗 **tall** [tɔːl] ⇔short
　〖(山や建物が)高い〗 **high** [hai] ⇔low

だから **because** [bikɔ́ːz]

たからもの〖宝物〗 **treasure** [tréʒər]

だきしめる〖抱きしめる〗 **hug** [hʌg]

たくさん **many** [méni], **much** [mʌtʃ]
　➡ 私には友達がたくさんいます。 *I have many friends.*
　➡ 冬には雪がたくさん降ります。 *We have much snow in the winter.*

タクシーうんてんしゅ〖タクシー運転手〗 **taxi driver** [tǽksi dràivər]

たこ〖凧〗 **kite** [kait]

タコ **octopus** [áktəpəs]

たしかめる〖確かめる〗 **make sure** [meik ʃúər]
　➡ 全部持っているかどうか確かめなさい。 *Make sure that you have everything with you.*

だす〖(～を出す)〗 **take out...** [teik aut], **hand in...** [hænd in], **mail** [meil]
　◉ 教科書を取り出す *take out the textbook*
　➡ レポートを出しなさい。 *Hand in your report.*
　➡ この手紙を出してください。 *Mail this letter, please.*

たすうの〖多数の〗 **many** [méni]　= おおい, たくさんの

たずねる **ask** [æsk]　= きく, たのむ

たたかう〖戦う〗 **fight** [fait] 過去形 fought [fɔːt]

ただしい〖正しい〗 **right** [rait]　⇔wrong まちがった
　➡ あなたはいつも正しい。 *You are always right.*

ただの **free** [friː]　= むりょうの, じゆうな, ひまな

ただひとつの〖ただ一つの〗 **only** [óunli]　= たった

たつ〖立つ〗 **stand** [stænd] 過去形 stood [stud]
　➡ つま先で立てますか？ *Can you stand on your toes?*

たっきゅう〖卓球〗 **table tennis** [téibl tènis]

たった **only** [óunli]　= ただひとつの

～だった **were** [wər] = ～にいた　weren't ～でなかった

たてもの〖建物〗 **building** [bíldiŋ]

たてる〖建てる〗 **build** [bild] 過去形 built [bilt]

たとえば **for example** [fər igzǽmpl]

たのしい〖楽しい〗 **happy** [hǽpi], **fun** [fʌn]

たのしいときをすごす〖楽しい時を過ごす〗 **have a good time**

たのしむ〖楽しむ〗 **enjoy** [indʒɔ́i]

たのむ〖頼む〗 **ask** [æsk]　= きく, たずねる

タバコをすう〖タバコを吸う〗 **smoke** [smouk]　= けむ

たび〖旅〗 **travel** [trǽvəl]　= trip [trip]　= りょこうす

たびたび〖度々〗 **often** [ɔːfn]　= よく, しょっちゅう

たぶん **maybe** [méibiː], **perhaps** [pərhǽps]

たべもの〖食べ物〗 **food** [fuːd]

たべる〖食べる〗 **eat** [iːt] 過去形 ate [eit]
　〖食べる〗 **have** [hæv, həv] 過去形 had [həd]
　◉ 朝食をとる = have breakfast
　➡ 私は昼食にハンバーガーを食べました。 *I had a hamburger for lunch.*

たまご〖卵〗 **egg** [eg]　◉ ゆでたまご = boiled egg

だます **cheat** [tʃiːt]　= カンニングをする

だまった〖黙った〗 **silent** [sáilənt], **quiet** [kwáiit] ⇔nois

　➡ だまりなさい！ *Be quiet!*

たまに～ **seldom** [séldəm]　= めったに～しない

タマネギ **onion** [ʌ́njen]

ためす【試す】 **try** [trai] ＝〜しようとする

たりょうの【多量の】 **much** [mʌtʃ] ＝おおい, たくさん

だれ **who** [hu:]

➡ 誰がお休みですか？ *Who is absent?*

だれか **someone** [sʌ́mwʌn]

だれでも **everyone** [évriwʌn] ＝みんな

だれの **whose** [hu:z]

➡ これは誰のかばんですか？ *Whose bag is this?*

たんご【単語】 **word** [wə:rd]

たんさんいんりょう【炭酸飲料】 **pop** [pɑp]

だんし【男子】 **boy** [bɔi] ＝おとこのこ

たんじゅんな【単純な】 **simple** [simpl]

たんじょうする【誕生する】 **be born** [bi bɔ:rn]

たんじょうび【誕生日】 **birthday** [bə́:rθdei]

たんす **chest** [tʃest] ＝むね

たんにん【担任】 **homeroom teacher**
[hóumrù:m tí:tʃər]

ちこくする【〜に遅刻する】 **be late for...** [bi léit fər]

➡ 私は授業に遅れました。 *I was late for class.*

ちず【地図】 **map** [mæp], **atlas** [ǽtləs]

ちち【父】 **father** [fá:ðər] ＝おとうさん

ちゃいろ【茶色】 **brown** [braun]

〜ちゅう【〜中】 **during** [dú(:)riŋ] ＝（〜の）あいだに

ちゅういぶかい【注意深い】 **careful** [kéərfəl]

ちゅういぶかく【注意深く】 **carefully** [kéərfəli]

ちゅうがく【中学】 **junior high school**
[dʒu:njər hái sku:l] ● 高校＝high school

ちゅうしゃじょう【駐車場】 **parking lot** [pá:rkiŋ lɑt]

ちゅうしん【中心】 **the center** [séntər] ＝まんなか

ちゅうもんする【注文する】 **order** [ɔ́:rdər] ＝めいれい

ちょうれい【朝礼】 **morning assembly**
[mɔ́:rniŋ əsémbli]

チョーク **chalk** [tʃɔ:k]

ちらかった **messy** [mési]

# ち　チ

ち【血】 **blood** [blʌd] ● 血液型＝blood type

ちいさい【小さい】 **little** [litl] ＝すこししかない
【小さい】 **small** [smɔ:l] ⇔ big 大きい
【小さい】 **low** [low] （声が小さい）

ちかい【近い】 **near** [niər], **close** [klous] ＝ちかくに

➡ もっと近くに来なさい。 *Come closer.*

ちがいない【違いない】 **must** [mʌst, məst]
＝〜しなければならない　mustn't 〜してはいけない

➡ 彼は金持ちに違いない。 *He must be rich.*

ちがう【違う】 **different** [díf(ə)rənt]
**wrong** [wrɔ:ŋ]

➡ ぼくの答えは君のと違っている。 *My answer is different from yours.*

ちかくに【近くに】 **near** [niər], **close** [klous] ＝ちかい

ちかてつ【地下鉄】 **subway** [sʌ́bwei]

● イギリスでは underground と言います。

ちきゅう【地球】 **the earth** [ə:rθ]

➡ 地球は太陽の周りを回っています。 *The earth goes around the sun.*

ちきゅうぎ【地球儀】 **globe** [glʌb]

チケット **ticket** [tíkit] ＝きっぷ

# つ　ツ

（〜に）ついて **about** [əbáut] ＝およそ, やく

つうがくようかばん【通学用かばん】 **school bag**

つかう【（〜を）使う】 **use** [ju:z], **spend** [spend]
過去形 spent [spent] （spend は時間やお金を使う）

➡ いくら使えるの？ *How much can you spend?*

➡ かさを借りてもいいですか？ *May I use your umbrella?*

（〜を）つかまえる **catch** [kætʃ] 過去形 caught [kɔ:t]

つかれた【疲れた】 **tired** [táiərd]

つかれる【疲れる】 **be tired** [táiərd], **get tired**

➡ 私は疲れました。 *I am tired. I got tired.*

つき【月】 **moon** [mu:n], **month** [mʌnθ]

➡ 1年は12か月あります。 *There are twelve months in a year.*

つぎつぎと【次々と】 **one after another**
[wʌn æftər ənʌ́ðər]

つく【着く】 **reach** [ri:tʃ] ＝とうちゃくする

つくえ【机】 **desk** [desk]

つくる【（〜を）作る】 **make** [meik] 過去形 made [meid]

● ベッドを整える＝make the bed

● 物音を立てる＝make (a) noise [nɔ́iz]

つける **turn on** [tə:ⁿn ɔn], **keep** [ki:p]
- 明かりをつける＝turn on the light
- 日記をつける＝keep a diary

つたえる【伝える】 **tell** [tel] ＝はなす 過去形 **told** [tould]
→ スミス先生に私が病気でねこんでいると伝えてください。 *Please tell Ms. Smith that I am sick in bed.*

つづく【続く】 **continue** [kəntínju:]

つま【妻】 **wife** [waif]

つゆ【梅雨】 **the rainy season** [ðə réini sì:zn]

つよい【強い】 **strong** [strɔ(:)ŋ] ⇔ weak

つりせん **change** [tʃeindʒ] ＝かえる, のりかえる
→ はい, おつり（です）。 *Here is your change.*

つるす **hang** [hæŋ] ＝かける, ぶらさがる

つれてくる【連れて来る】 **bring** [briŋ] 過去形 **brought** [brɔːt]

# て テ

て【手】 **hand(s)** [hænd(z)] ＝わたす, くばる

～であった **was** [waz, wəs] ＝～にいた
wasn't ～でなかった
→ この家は空き家になっていた。昨日はそうではなかった（けど）。 *The house was empty. It wasn't yesterday.*

～である **am** [waz, wəs] 過去形 **was** [waz, wəs]

ていしゅつする【提出する】 **hand** [hænd] ＝くばる, わたす
→ 宿題を提出してください。 *Please hand in your homework.*

ティッシュペーパー **tissue** [tíʃu:]

テーブル **table** [teibl]

てがみ【手紙】 **letter** [létər] ＝もじ

できた **could** [kud, kəd] can の過去形
couldn't ～できなかった
→ テストを終わらせることができなかった。 *I couldn't finish the test.*

できる **can** [kæn, kən] ＝かん
→ 私は英語がじょうずに話せます。 *I can speak English well.*

でぐち【出口】 **exit** [égzit]

デザート **dessert** [dizə́ːrt]

でしょう **will** [wil, wəl]
→ 明日は寒いでしょう。でも雪は降らないでしょう。 *It will be cold tomorrow, but it won't snow.*

てつだう【（～を）手伝う】 **help** [help]
→ 私の宿題を手伝ってくれませんか? *Will you help me with my homework?*

てつぼう【鉄棒】 **horizontal bar** [hɔ́(:)rəzántəl baːr]

でない **not** [nɑt] ＝～しない

テニス **tennis** [ténis]

デパート **department store** [dipáːrtmənt stɔ̀ːr]

でも **but** [bʌt, bət]

テレビ **television** [télətvìʒən], **TV** [tíːvíː]

テレビゲーム **video game** [vídiòu geim]

てをたたく【手をたたく】 **clap** [klæp]

てをふる【手を振る】 **wave** [weiv] ＝なみ

てんき【天気】 **weather** [wéðər]
→ 天気はどうですか? *How is the weather?*

でんきスタンド【電気スタンド】 **lamp** [læmp]

でんきの【電気の】 **electric** [iléktrik]

てんきのよい【天気の良い】 **sunny** [sʌ́ni] ＝ひがてっている
→ 今日は天気が良くて暑いです。 *It is sunny and hot today.*

でんしゃ【電車】 **train** [trein]
- 電車の駅＝train station [stéiʃn]
- 電車の1両目＝the first car of the train

てんじょう【天井】 **ceiling** [síːliŋ]
- 天井の電気＝ceiling light

でんとう【電灯】 **light** [lait] ＝あかり, あかるい, かるい
- 電球＝light bulb [bʌlb]

テントウムシ **ladybug** [léidibʌ̀g]

でんわ【電話】 **telephone** [téləfoun], **phone** [foun
- 電話ボックス＝phone booth [buːs]
- けいたい電話＝cellular phone
- 留守番電話＝answering machine
→ 電話に出て! *Please answer the phone!*

でんわをかける【電話をかける】 **call** [kɔːl] ＝よぶ
→ あとで電話してください。 *Please call me later.*

# と ト

ドア **door** [dɔːr]

どうぞ **please** [pliːz]

とうちゃくする【到着する】 **arrive at** [əráiv ət], **get to** [gət tə], **reach** [riːtʃ]

→ 10分で羽田空港に着きます。 *I will arrive at Haneda airport in ten minutes.*

どうぶつ【動物】 **animal** [ǽnəməl]

どうぶつえん【動物園】 **zoo** [zu:]

とうもろこし **corn** [kɔ:rn]

どうろ【道路】 **road** [roud] ＝みち

とおり【通り】 **street** [stri:t]

トカゲ **lizard** [lízərd]

ときどき【時々】 **sometimes** [sʌ́mtaimz] ＝ことがある

とくいである【得意である】 **be good at...**

→ 私はスキーが得意です。 *I am good at skiing.*

過去形 **was good at...**

とくてん【得点】 **score** [skɔ:r], **point** [pɔint]

◉ 得点2対1＝a score of 2 to 1

→ 彼女は満点をとった。 *She got a perfect score.*

とくべつな **special** [spéʃəl]

とけい【時計】 **clock** [klɑk] （置時計, かけ時計）

**watch** [watʃ] （うで時計）

どこ **where** [hwéər]

→ どこに住んでいますか? *Where do you live?*

としとった【年取った】 **old** [ould] ＝ふるい

としょかん【図書館】 **library** [láibrəri]

とだな【戸棚】 **closet** [klázit] ＝おしいれ

とちゅうで【途中で】 **on the way**

どちら **which** [hwitʃ] ＝どれ

→ あなたのカバンはどっちですか? *Which is your bag?*

どちらも **both** [bouθ]

→ 犬も猫も好きです。 *I like both dogs and cats.*

どちらも〜ない **not either... or...**

→ 犬も猫も好きではありません。 *I do not like either dogs or cats.*

ドッジボール **dodgeball** [dádʒbɔ̀:l]

とつぜん【突然】 **suddenly** [sʌ́dnli] ＝きゅうに

とても **very** [véri] ＝ひじょうに

→ 私は英語がとても好きです。 *I like English very well.*

→ 私は彼のことをよく知っています。 *I know him very well.*

となりの **next door** [nekst dɔ:r]

どのくらい **how far** [hau fá:r] （きょり）

**how long** [hau lɔ́:ŋ] （長さ）

→ 家から駅までどれくらいの距離ですか? *How far is the station from your house?*

→ 学校まで時間はどれくらいかかりますか? *How long does it take you to get to school?*

どのように **how** [hau]

→ 学校にどのように来ていますか? *How do you come to school?*

とぶ【飛ぶ】 **fly** [flai] 過去形 **flew** [flu:]

【跳ぶ】 **hop** [hɑp] （片足で軽く） ＝はねる

【跳ぶ】 **jump** [dʒʌmp] ＝ジャンプする

トマト **tomato** [təméitou]

とまる【止まる】 **stop** [stɑp] ＝やめる

→ 赤信号では止まりなさい。 *Stop at red lights.*

ともだち【友達】 **friend** [frend]

どようび【土曜日】 **Saturday** [sǽtərdei]

トラ **tiger** [táigər]

トラック **truck** [trʌk]

トリ【鳥】 **bird** [bə:rd]

どりょく【努力】 **effort** [éfərt]

◉ 努力する＝make an effort

とる【取る】 **take** [teik] 過去形 **took** [tuk]

【取る】 **get** [get] 過去形 **got** [gɑt]

【盗る】 **steal** [sti:l] ＝ぬすむ 過去形 **stole** [stoul]

【捕る】 **catch** [kætʃ] 過去形 **caught** [kɔ:t]

→ 3枚ずつカードを取ってください。 *Please take three cards each.*

→ ぼくはちょうちょを3びき捕ったよ。 *I caught three butterflies.*

ドル（$） **dollar** [dálər]

トレー **tray** [trei] （お盆）

ドレス **dress** [dres]

どれ **which** [witʃ] ＝どちら

どれでも **any** [éni] ＝いくつかの, （否定文で）すこしも〜ない

どろ【泥】 **mud** [mʌd]

どろぼう【泥棒】 **thief** [θi:f]

トンボ **dragonfly** [drǽgənflai]

## な ナ

ない **no** [nou] ＝いいえ

→ 今日は宿題がない。 *I have no homework today.*

ナイフ **knife** [naif]

なおす〔直す〕 **fix** [fiks] ＝こていする

→ パンクした自転車のタイヤをなおすことができるの？ *Can you fix a flat tire on a bicycle?*

なかに〔〜の中に〕 **in** [in]

→ 教科書をかばんの中に入れなさい。 *Put your textbook in your bag.*

ながい〔長い〕 **long** [lɔːŋ] ⇔ short みじかい

なかみのない〔中身のない〕 **empty** [émpti] ＝からの

なく〔泣く〕 **cry** [krai] ＝さけぶ

なくす **lose** [luːz] 過去形 lost [lɔ(:)st] ＝まける
**missing** [mísiŋ]

→ カメラをなくした。 *I lost my camera.*

→ さいふがない！ *My wallet is missing!*

なげる〔投げる〕 **throw** [θrou] 過去形 threw [θruː]

〜なしで **without** [wiðáut]

なぜ **why** [hwai]

→ なぜ英語が好きなのですか？ *Why do you like English?*

なつ〔夏〕 **summer** [sʌ́mər]

なづける〔名づける〕 **name** [neim] ＝なまえ

なに〔何〕 **what** [hwat]

→ あなたの名前は何といいますか？ *What is your name?*

なにか〔何か〕 **something** [sʌ́mθiŋ]

なにも〜ない〔何も〜ない〕 **nothing** [nʌ́θiŋ]

なべ〔（浅い）なべ〕 **pan** [pæn] ＝フライパン
〔（深い）なべ〕 **pot** [pat]

なまえ〔名前〕 **name** [neim] ＝なづける

なまける〔怠ける〕 **be lazy** [léizi]

→ 怠けてはいけません。 *Don't be lazy.*

なみ〔波〕 **wave** [weiv] ＝てをふる

なみだ〔涙〕 **tear** [tíər] ＝やぶる

なやむ〔悩む〕 **worry about** [wə́ːri əbàut]

ならう〔習う〕 **learn** [ləːrn]

ならぶ〔並ぶ〕 **line up** [láin ʌ̀p] ＝れつにならぶ

→ 並びなさい。 *Stand in line.*

なわとび〔なわ跳び〕 **jump rope** [dʒʌ́mp ròup]

→ 私はなわ跳びで100回跳ぶことができます。
*I can jump rope (for) one hundred times.*

なんさい〔何歳（年齢）〕 **how old** [hàu óuld]

→ あなたの学校は創立して何年ですか？ *How old is your school?*

なんじ〔何時〕 **what time** [hwàt táim]

→ 朝はいつも何時に起きますか？ *What time do you usually get up in the morning?*

# に　ニ

〜にいる〔（場所）にいる〕 **be in...**

〜にいた **was** [waz, wəz]（〜だった） am の過去形
**were** [wəːr, wər]（〜だった） are の過去形
wasn't, weren't 〜でなかった

→ 私は2日前沖縄にいました。 *I was in Okinawa two days ago.*

〜にいる **am** [æm, əm], **are** [aːr, ər], **is** [iz]

においがする〔匂いがする，匂う〕 **smell** [smel]

→ これはいいにおいがします。 *This smells good.*

にかいに〔2階に〕 **upstairs** [ʌpstéərz]

→ 2階に行きなさい。 *Go upstairs.*

にがつ〔2月〕 **February** [fébruəri]

にぎる〔握る〕 **hold** [hould] ＝もつ 過去形 held [held]

にく〔肉〕 **meat** [miːt]

にげる〔逃げる〕 **run away** [rʌn əwéi]

に, さん（の）〔2, 3（の）〕 **a few** [ə fjuː]

にし〔西〕 **west** [west]

→ 太陽は西にしずむ。 *The sun sets in the west.*

にじ〔虹〕 **rainbow** [réinbou]

にちようび〔日曜日〕 **Sunday** [sʌ́ndei]

にっき〔日記〕 **diary** [dáiəri]

にっこりわらう〔（にっこり）笑う〕 **smile** [smail] ＝ほほえむ

→ 私ににっこり笑ってください。 *Please smile at me*

にど〔2度〕 **twice** [twais] ＝にばい

にど（と）〔2度（と）〕 **again** [əgén]

→ 2度としてはいけません。 *Don't do it again.*

〜になる **become** [bikʌ́m] 過去形 became [bikéim]

にばい〔2倍〕 **twice** [twais] ＝にど

にほん〔日本〕 **Japan** [dʒəpǽn]

にほんご〔日本語〕 **Japanese** [dʒæpəníːz] ＝こくご

にゅうがく〔入学〕 **entrance** [éntrəns]

● 入学式 ＝ entrance ceremony [sérəmòuni]

ニュース **news** [njuːz]

にる〔似る〕 **look like...** [lúk làik]

➡ 彼はサルに似ている。　*He looks like a monkey.*

にる【煮る】 **boil** [bɔil]

にわ【庭】 **garden** [gáːrdən] （花や木をそろえた庭）

**yard** [jɑːrd] ● 校庭＝school yard

にんきのある【人気のある】 **popular** [pápjulər]

にんぎょう【人形】 **doll** [dɑl]

にんげん【人間】 **man** [mæn] ＝おとこのひと

**human being** [hjúːmən bíːiŋ]

にんじん　**carrot** [kǽrət]

# ぬ ヌ

ぬぐ【（シャツなどを）脱ぐ】 **take off...** [teik ɔf]

過去形 **took off** [tuk ɔf]

➡ シャツを脱ぎなさい。　*Take off your shirt.*

ぬすむ【盗む】 **steal** [stiːl] ＝とる 過去形 **stole** [stoul]

ぬらす【濡らす】 **wet** [wet] ＝ぬれた 過去形 **wet** [wet]（同形）

ぬる　**paint** [peint]（ペンキでぬる）, **color** [kʌ́lər]（色をぬる）

➡ このつくえを白にぬってください。　*Please paint this desk white.*

ぬれた【濡れた】 **wet** [wet] ⇔ dry

➡ ぬれちゃった。　*I got wet.*

# ね ネ

ね【根】 **root** [ruːt]

ねがう【願う】 **wish** [wiʃ], **hope** [houp] ＝きたいする, のぞむ

ネクタイ　**tie** [tai] ＝むすぶ

ネコ　**cat** [kæt]（鳴き声はmeow） ● 子ネコ＝kitten

ネズミ　**mouse** [maus] 複数形 **mice** [mais], **rat** [ræt]

● mouse はハツカネズミ。rat より小さい。（鳴き声は squeak [skwiːk]）

ねだん【値段】 **price** [prais]

ねつ【熱】 **heat** [hiːt], **fever** [fíːvər]（病気の熱）

➡ 熱が高い。　*I have a high fever.*

ねぼうする【寝坊する】 **oversleep** [òuvərslíːp]

過去形 **overslept** [òuvərslépt]

ねむい【眠い】 **sleepy** [slíːpi]

➡ 私は眠いです。　*I am sleepy.*

ねむる【眠る】 **sleep** [sliːp] 過去形 **slept** [slept]

➡ よく眠れましたか？　*Did you sleep well?*

➡ 全然寝ていません。　*I did not sleep at all.*

ねる【寝る】 **go to bed** [góu tə bed]

過去形 **went to bed** [wént tə bed]

➡ もう寝なくてはいけません。　*You have to go to bed now.*

ねん【年】 **year** [jiər]

➡ この建物は設立100年です。　*This building is one hundred years old.*

# の ノ

のうぎょう【農業】 **farming** [fáːrmiŋ]

のうじょう【農場】 **farm** [fɑːrm]

のうふ【農夫】 **farmer** [fáːrmər]

ノート　**notebook** [nóutbuk]

のぞむ【望む】 **hope** [houp] ＝きたいする, ねがう

➡ 医者になりたいと思っています。　*I hope to be a doctor.*

➡ 私はまたあなたに会いたいです。　*I hope to see you again.*

ノックする　**knock** [nɑk]

➡ ドアをノックしてください。*Please knock on the door.*

のっていく【乗って行く】 **take** [teik] 過去形 **took** [tuk]

のど　**throat** [θrout]

のどがかわいた【のどが渇いた】 **thirsty** [θə́ːrsti]

のばす【伸ばす】 **stretch** [stretʃ]

➡ 体を伸ばしましょう。　*Let's stretch out.*

のばす【延ばす】 **put off** [put ɔf] （＝延期する）

のぼる【登る】 **climb** [klaim], **go up** [gou ʌp]

【昇る】 **rise** [raiz] ＝あがる

● 木に登る＝climb a tree

のみもの【飲み物】 **drink** [driŋk]

のむ【飲む】 **drink** [driŋk] 過去形 **drank** [dræŋk]

【飲む】 **take** [teik] 過去形 **took** [tuk]

➡ 毎食後に2つぶずつ薬を飲みなさい。　*Take two tablets after each meal.*

のようだ　**seem** [siːm] ＝らしい

のり【糊】 **paste** [peist], **glue** [gluː]

のりかえる　**change** [tʃeindʒ]

➡ 次の駅で電車をのりかえましょう。　*Let's change trains at the next station.*

のる〔乗る〕 **get on...** [get ɑn] (バスや電車に) 過去形 **got on**
**ride** [raid] (自転車や馬に) 過去形 **rode** [roud]
**take** [teik] 過去形 **took** [tuk]

→ バスに乗りましょう。 *Let's get on the bus.*

→ 私は一輪車に乗ることができます。 *I can ride a unicycle.*

→ 街へ行くのに電車に乗りました。 *We took a train to the city.*

# は ハ

は〔葉〕 **leaf** [li:f] 複数形 **leaves** [li:vs]

は〔歯〕 **tooth** [tu:θ] 複数形 **teeth** [ti:θ]

● 歯ブラシ = toothbrush [túːθbrʌʃ]

● 歯みがき粉 = toothpaste [túːθpèist]

パーティー **party** [páːrti]

バーベキュー **barbecue** [báːrbəkjùː]

はい **yes** [jes], **here** [hiər] (名前を呼ばれた時, 自分がここにいると答える時に使う)

バイオリン **violin** [vàiəlín]

ハイキング **hiking** [háikiŋ]

はいしゃ〔歯医者〕 **dentist** [déntist]

パイナップル **pineapple** [páinæpl]

はいる〔入る〕 **join** [jɔin], **come in**

→ 私もなかまに入っていいですか? *May I join you?*

→ 中に入っていいですか? *May I come in?*

ハガキ **postcard** [póustkàːrd] = ポストカード

ばかな **silly** [síli], **foolish** [fúːliʃ]

はくしゅ(する)〔拍手(する)〕 **give...a big hand**

→ 彼に大きな拍手を送りましょう。 *Let's give him a big hand.*

はけ **brush** [brʌʃ] = ブラシ

はげます **encourage** [inkɔ́ːridʒ]

はこ〔箱〕 **box** [bɑks]

はこぶ〔運ぶ〕 **carry** [kǽri]

はさみ **scissors** [sízərz] (必ずsが付きます)

→ はさみでこの紙を半分に切ってください。 *Cut this paper in half with scissors.*

はし〔橋〕 **bridge** [bridʒ]

はし〔端〕 **end** [end]

● ロープの両端 = both ends of the rope

はじまる〔始まる, 始める〕 **begin** [bigín] 過去形 **began** [bigǽn]
**start** [stɑːrt] = しゅっぱつする

→ はじめましょう。 *Let's begin.*

はじめて〔初めて〕 **for the first time**

→ 私は初めて東京に行った。 *I went to Tokyo for the first time.*

はじめに **first of all**

はじめまして **Nice to meet you.**

パジャマ **pajamas** [pədʒáːməz] (必ずsが付きます)

ばしょ〔場所〕 **place** [pleis]

はしる〔走る〕 **run** [rʌn] 過去形 **ran** [ræn]

→ 学校まで走って行こう。 *Let's run to school.*

バス **bus** [bʌs] ● バス停 = bus stop [stɑp]

● バスに乗る = take a bus

バスケットボール **basketball** [bǽskitbɔ̀ːl]

→ バスケットボールをしよう。 *Let's play basketball.*

はた〔旗〕 **flag** [flæg]

はたらく〔働く〕 **work** [wəːrk] = べんきょうする, しごと

はちがつ〔8月〕 **August** [ɔ́ːgəst]

はっけんする〔発見する〕 **discover** [diskʌ́vər]

バッタ **grasshopper** [grǽshɑ̀pər]

はつめいする〔発明する〕 **invent** [invént]

バドミントン **badminton** [bǽdmintən]

はな〔花〕 **flower** [fláuər]

● アサガオ = morning glory [mɔ́ːrniŋ glɔ́ːri], コスモス = cosmos [kázməs], サクラ = cherry blossoms [tʃéri blɑ̀səm], スイセン = daffodil [dǽfədil], タンポポ = dandelion [dǽndəlàiən], チューリップ = tulip [tjúːlip], バラ = rose [rouz], ヒマワリ = sunflower [sʌ́nflàuər], ユリ = lily [líli]

はな〔鼻〕 **nose** [nouz]

はなしあう〔話し合う〕 **discuss** [diskʌ́s]

はなす〔話す〕 **speak** [spiːk] 過去形 **spoke** [spouk]
〔話す〕 **tell** [tel] 過去形 **told** [tould] = つたえる
〔話す〕 **talk** [tɔːk] = しゃべる

→ この部屋で大声で話さないでください。 *Don't speak loudly in this room.*

→ あなたの家族のことを教えてください。 *Please tell me about your family.*

バナナ **banana** [bənǽnə]

はなび〔花火〕 **fireworks** [fáiərwə̀ːrks]

はなや【花屋】 **florist** [flɔ́:rist]

はね【羽】 **wing** [wíŋ]（つばさ）, **feather** [féðər]（羽毛）

はねる【跳ねる】 hop [hap] ＝とぶ 過去形 hopped [hapt]

はは【母】 **mother** [mʌ́ðər] ＝おかあさん

パパ **dad** [dæd]

はやい【速い】 **fast** [fæst]（速度が）⇔slow
　　　　　　　 **quick** [kwik]（行動や動作が）⇔slow

はやく【早く】 **early** [ə́:rli]（時期が）⇔late
　　　　　　　 **quickly** [kwíkli]（すばやく）⇔slowly
➡ 明日は学校に早く行かなければいけません。 *I have to go to school early tomorrow morning.*

はる【春】 **spring** [spriŋ]

バレーボール **volleyball** [válibɔ̀:l]

はれた【晴れた】 **fine** [fain], **clear** [kliər], **sunny** [sʌ́ni]

パン **bread** [bred]

ばん【番（順番）】 **turn** [tə:rn] ＝まわす, まわる
➡ あなたがしゃべる番です。 *It's your turn to speak.*

ハンカチ **handkerchief** [hǽŋkərtʃi(:)f]

ばんぐみ【番組】 **program** [próugræm]

パンケーキ **pancakes** [pǽnkèiks]

ばんごう【番号】 **number** [nʌ́mbər] ＝かず

ハンサムな **handsome** [hǽnsəm]
➡ 彼はとてもハンサムです。 *He is so handsome.*

パンダ **panda** [pǽndə]

はんたいの【反対の】 **opposite** [ápəzit]

はんにん【犯人】 **criminal** [krímini]

ハンバーガー **hamburger** [hǽmbə:rgər]

はんぶん（の）【半分（の）】 **half** [hæf, ha:f]

ハンマー **hammer** [hǽmər] ＝かなづち

パンや【パン屋】 **bakery** [béikəri]

# ひ ヒ

ひ【日】 **day** [dei], **date** [deit], **the sun** [ðə sʌ́n]
➡ 今日は何曜日ですか? *What day (of the week) is it today?*

ひ【火】 **fire** [fáiər]

ピアノ **piano** [piǽnou]

ビーだま【ビー玉】 **marble(s)** [ma:rbl(z)]

ピーマン **green pepper** [grí:n pèpər]

ビール **beer** [biər]

ひがてっている【日が照っている】 **sunny** [sʌ́ni]
　＝てんきのよい, はれた

ひく【（楽器を）弾く】 **play** [plei] ＝あそぶ, する
➡ 私はピアノを弾くことができます。 *I can play the piano.*

ひく **pull** [pul]（引く）⇔push 押す
　　 **catch** [kætʃ]（かぜをひく）過去形 caught [kɔ:t]
　　 **have** [hæv, həv]（かぜをひいている）
　　 過去形 had [hæd, həd]
➡ ドアを開けるにはドアノブを引かなければいけません。 *You have to pull the door knob to open the door.*
➡ かぜをひきました。 *I caught a cold.*
➡ かぜをひいています。 *I have a cold.*

ひくい【低い】 **low** [lou]（高さが）⇔high
　　　　　　 【低い】 **short** [ʃɔ:rt] ＝みじかい ⇔long

ピクニック **picnic** [píknik]

ひこうき【飛行機】 **plane** [plein], **airplane** [éərplèin]
　◉ ジェット機＝jet [dʒet]

ひざ【膝】 **knee(s)** [ni:(z)]

ピザ **pizza** [pí:tsə]

ひじかけいす【肘掛け椅子】 **armchair** [á:rmtʃèər]

びじゅつかん【美術館】 **art museum** [mju:zí:əm]

ひじょうに【非常に】 **very** [véri] ＝とても
➡ 私は英語がとても好きです。 *I like English very much.*

ひたい **forehead** [fɔ́:rid]

ひだりの【左の】 **left** [left] ⇔right 右の
➡ 左手をあげなさい。 *Raise your left hand.*

ひっかく **scratch** [skrætʃ]

びっくりする **be surprised** [bi: sərpráizd] ＝おどろく
➡ びっくりした! *I'm surprised!*

ひづけ【日付】 **date** [deit] ＝ひ
➡ 今日はなんにちですか? *What is the date today?*

ひっこす【引っ越す】 **move** [mu:v] ＝うごく, かんどうする
➡ 来月東京に引っ越します。 *I will move to Tokyo next month.*

ヒツジ **sheep** [ʃi:p] 単複同形 sheep [ʃi:p]

ひつようとする【必要とする】 **need** [ni:d]
➡ 私には辞書が必要です。 *I need a dictionary.*

は
ひ

23

ひときれ〖一切れ〗 **piece** [pi:s] ＝かけら

ひとびと〖人々〗 **people** [pi:pl]

ひとりで〖一人で〗 **alone** [əlóun]

ひまな〖暇な〗 **free** [fri:] ＝ただの, じゆうな, むりょうの

ひみつ〖秘密(の)〗 **secret** [sí:krit]

びょう〖秒〗 **second** [sékənd] (＝2番目の)

びょういん〖病院〗 **hospital** [háspitəl]

びょうきの〖病気の〗 **sick** [sik], **ill** [il]

→ お母さんは病気で寝込んでいます。 *My mother is sick in bed.*

ひょうげんする〖表現する〗 **express** [iksprés] ＝そくたつ, きゅうこう

ヒヨコ **chick** [tʃik]

ひらく〖開く〗 **open** [óupən] ＝あける

ひる〖昼〗 **afternoon** [æftərnú:n]

ひるごはん〖昼ごはん〗 **lunch** [lʌntʃ]

ひるねをする〖昼寝をする〗 **take a nap** [teik ə næp] 過去形 **took a nap** [tuk ə næp]

ひるやすみ〖昼休み〗 **lunch break** [lʌntʃ brèik]

ひろい〖広い〗 **wide** [waid] (幅が広い) **large** [lɑ:rdʒ] (面積が広い)

ひろいあげる〖拾い上げる〗 **pick up...** [pik əp]

ピンク **pink** [piŋk]

びんぼうな〖貧乏な〗 **poor** [puər] ⇔ **rich** 金持ちの

## ふ フ

ふうふ〖夫婦〗 **couple** [kʌpl]

プール **swimming pool** [swímiŋ pu:l]

フェリー **ferry** [féri]

フォーク **fork** [fo:rk]

ふかい〖深い〗 **deep** [di:p]

ふく〖服〗 **clothes** [klouz]

ふく〖拭く〗 **wipe** [waip] (机などをふく, ふきとる)

ふく〖吹く〗 **blow** [blou] (風が吹く) 過去形 **blew** [blu:] 〖吹く〗 **whistle** [hwisl] (口笛を吹く)

ふくつう〖腹痛〗 **stomachache** [stʌ́məkèik]

→ おなかがいたい。 *I have a stomachache.*

～ふじん〖～夫人〗 **Mrs.** [mísiz]

ブタ **pig** [pig]

ふたご〖双子〗 **twins** [twinz]

ふつうは〖普通は〗 **usually** [jú:ʒuəli] ＝いつもは

ぶつける **bump** [bʌmp]

→ 頭をドアにぶつけた。 *I bumped my head on the door.*

ふっとうする〖沸騰する〗 **boil** [boil] ＝ゆでる, わかす

ふでばこ〖筆箱〗 **pencil case** [pénsəl kèis]

ブドウ **grape(s)** [greip(s)] (通常はsを付けてgrapes)

ふとった〖太った〗 **fat** [fæt] ⇔ **thin** やせた

ふとる〖太る〗 **get fat** [get fæt] ⇔ **lose weight** やせる

ふね〖舟〗 **rowboat** [róubòut] ＝ボート 〖船〗 **ship** [ʃip]

ふゆ〖冬〗 **winter** [wíntər]

フライトアテンダント **flight attendant** [fláit ətèndənt] (航空機の客室乗務員)

フライドチキン **fried chicken** [fráid tʃíkin]

フライパン **pan** [pæn] ＝(浅い)なべ

→ フライパンに油をひいて。 *Oil the pan.*

ブラウス **blouse** [blaus]

ぶらさがる **hang** [hæŋ] ＝かける 過去形 **hung** [hʌŋ]

ブラシ **brush** [brʌʃ] ＝はけ

ブランコ **swing** [swiŋ] ＝ゆれる

ふる〖振る〗 **shake** [ʃeik] 過去形 **shook** [ʃuk] **swing** [swiŋ] 過去形 **swung** [swʌŋ]

ふるい〖古い〗 **old** [ould] ＝としとった

ブルーベリー **blueberry** [blú:bèri]

プレゼント **present** [prézənt]

ふれる **touch** [tʌtʃ] ＝さわる

ふろ〖風呂〗 **bath** [bæθ]

ふろにはいる〖風呂に入る〗 **take a bath** [téik ə bæθ] 過去形 **took a bath** [túk ə bæθ]

→ 今すぐお風呂に入りなさい。 *Take a bath right now.*

ふろば〖風呂場〗 **bathroom** [bæθrù:m] ＝おてあらい

ブロッコリー **broccoli** [brákəli]

ふん〖分〗 **minute** [mínit]

ぶんしょう〖文章〗 **sentence** [séntəns]

ふんすい〖噴水〗 **fountain** [fáuntən]

## へ ヘ

ヘアブラシ **hairbrush** [héərbrʌ̀ʃ]

へいき〖平気〗 **all right** [ó:l ràit] ＝だいじょうぶ

【平気】 **don't mind** [maind]

➡ ぼくは平気です。 *I'm all right.*

➡ かまわないよ。 *I don't mind.*

へいわ【平和】 **peace** [piːs]

べきである **should** [ʃud, ʃəd] ＝～すべき

ベーコン **bacon** [béikən]

　⚫ ベーコンエッグ＝bacon and eggs

ページ **page** [peidʒ]

へそ **bellybutton** [bélibÀtən]

へた【～が下手である】 **be poor at...** [púər ət]

➡ 私は絵を描くのが下手です。 *I am poor at drawing.*
過去形 was poor at [wəz púər ət]

ベッド **bed** [bed]

ペットボトル **plastic bottle** [plǽstik bὰtl]

ベッドをととのえる **make the bed** [méik ðə bèd]
過去形 made the bed [méid ðə bèd]

べつの【別の】 **another** [ənÁðər]

➡ 別のシャツを見せてください。 *Please show me another shirt.*

ヘビ **snake** [sneik]

へや【部屋】 **room** [ruːm]

ヘリコプター **helicopter** [hélikὰptər]

ベル **bell** [bel] ＝すず，かね

へんか（する）【変化（する）】 **change** [tʃeindʒ]

べんかい（する）【弁解（する）】 **excuse** [ikskjúːz]

　※「弁解」の意味の名詞では発音がかわります。excuse [ikskjúːs]

べんきょうする【勉強する】 **study** [stÁdi]

　　　　　　【勉強する】 **work** [wəːrk] ＝はたらく，しごと

➡ 水曜日は英語を勉強します。 *I study English on Wednesday.*

べんごし【弁護士】 **lawyer** [lɔ́ːjər]

へんじ【返事】 **answer** [ǽnsər] ＝こたえる

ベンチ **bench** [bentʃ]

へんな【変な】 **strange** [streindʒ]

べんりな【便利な】 **convenient** [kənvíːnjənt]

# ほ ホ

ぼう【棒】 **stick** [stik]，**bar** [bɑːr]

ぼうえんきょう【望遠鏡】 **telescope** [téləskòup]

ほうかご【放課後】 **after school** [ǽftər skuːl]

➡ 放課後友達と野球をします。 *I play baseball with my friends after school.*

ほうこう【方向】 **direction** [dirékʃən]

ほうこく（する）【報告（する）】 **report** [ripɔ́ːrt]

ぼうし【帽子】 **cap** [kæp] ＝やきゅうぼう
　　　　　　 **hat** [hæt] （ふちのある帽子）

ほうほう【方法】 **way** [wei] ＝みち，やりかた

ほうもんする【訪問する】 **visit** [vízit] ＝おとずれる

ボウリング **bowling** [bóuliŋ]

ホウレンソウ **spinach** [spínitʃ]

ほえる【吠える】 **bark** [bɑːrk]

ボート **boat** [bout]
　　　　 **rowboat** [róubòut]（こぎボート）＝ふね

ぼくたちの **our** [áuər] ＝わたしたちの

➡ 彼がぼくたちの先生です。 *He is our teacher.*

ぼくたちは（が） **we** [wiː, wi] ＝わたしたちは（が）

➡ ぼくたちは学生です。 *We are students.*

ぼくたちを（に） **us** [ʌs, əs] ＝わたしたちを（に）

➡ ぼくたちを知っていますか? *Do you know us?*

ぼくを（に） **me** [miː] ＝わたしを（に）

➡ ぼくに何か食べる物をください。 *Please give me something to eat.*

ぼくの **my** [mai] ＝わたしの

➡ これがぼくの家です。 *This is my house.*

ぼくは（が） **I** [ai] ＝わたしは（が）

➡ ぼくは学生です。 *I am a student.*

ポケット **pocket** [pάkit]

ほこり【誇り】 **pride** [praid]

ほこり **dust** [dʌst]

ほこりにおもう【（～を）誇りに思う】 **be proud of...** [práud əv]

➡ 私は自分の家族を誇りに思っています。 *I am proud of my family.*

ほし【星】 **star** [stɑːr]

ほしい **want** [wɑnt]

➡ 私は大きな犬がほしいです。 *I want a big dog.*

ほす【干す】 **dry** [drai] ＝かわいた，かわかす

ポストカード **postcard** [póustkὰːrd] ＝ハガキ

ほそい【細い】 **thin** [θin] ⇔ fat 太った

ボタン（をとめる） **button** [bÁtən]

➡ シャツのボタンをとめなさい。 *Button up your shirt.*

へ
ほ

25

ホッチキス　**stapler** [stéiplər]

→ ホッチキスはどこにある？　*Where is the stapler?*

ホッチキスでとめる　**staple** [stéipl]

→ これらの紙をホッチキスでとめてください。

*Please staple these papers.*

→ この部分とこの部分をホッチキスでとめなさい。

*Staple this part and this part together.*

ホットドッグ　**hot dog** [hát dɔ̀g]

ポテトフライ　**French fries** [frén tʃ fràiz]

（たっぷりの油で揚げたポテト）

ホテル　**hotel** [houtél]

ほとんど　**almost** [ɔ́:lmoust]

→ ほとんどの人が欠席した。　*Almost everyone was absent.*

ほほえむ【微笑む】　**smile** [smail]　＝ （にっこり）わらう

ほる【掘る】　**dig** [dig]　過去形 **dug** [dʌg]

ホワイトボード　**whiteboard** [hwáitbɔ̀:rd]

ほん【本】　**book** [buk]　＝ よやくする

ほんきの【本気の】　**serious** [síəriəs]　＝ まじめな

→ 本気ですか？　*Are you serious?*

ほんとうに【本当に】　**really** [ríəli]

→ 本当なの？　*Really?*

ほんとうの【本当の】　**real** [rí:əl, ríəl], **true** [tru:]

ほんとうのこと【本当のこと】　**truth** [tru:θ]

→ 本当のことを言って。　*Tell me the truth.*

# ま マ

まい～【毎～】　**every** [évri]　＝ ～ごと

まいにち【毎日】　**every day** [évri dei]

● 毎朝＝every morning　● 毎週＝every week

まいにちの【毎日の】　**everyday** [évridèi]

● 毎日のくらし　everyday life

まえに【前に】　**ago** [əgóu]（今から…前に）

**before** [bifɔ́:r]（～の前に，～する前に）

→ ぼくは3年前に東京に行きました。　*I went to Tokyo three years ago.*

→ 食べる前に手を洗いなさい。　*Wash your hands before you eat.*

まかす【負かす】　**beat** [bi:t]　過去形 **beat** [bi:t]（同形）

→ きみを負かすことができるよ！　*I can beat you!*

まくら【枕】　**pillow** [pílou]

まける【負ける】　**lose** [lu:z]　＝ なくす　過去形 **lost** [lɔst]

まご【孫】　**grandchild** [grǽntʃàild]

複数形 **grandchildren** [grǽntʃìldrən]

まじめな【真面目な】　**serious** [síəriəs]　＝ ほんきの

まじょ【魔女】　**witch** [witʃ]

まずしい【貧しい】　**poor** [puər]　⇔ **rich** 金持ちの

また　**again** [əgén]　＝ もういちど

まだ～ない　**not…yet** [jet]

まち【町】　**town** [taun]

まちがい【間違い】　**mistake** [mistéik]

まちがえる【間違える】　**make a mistake**

過去形 **made a mistake**

まちがった【間違った】　**wrong** [rɔ(:)ŋ] ⇔ **right** 正しい

→ あなたは間違っています。　*You are wrong.*

→ 電話番号がまちがっていますよ。　*You have the wrong number.*

まつ【待つ】　**wait** [weit]　● ～を待つ＝wait for…

**hold on** [hould ən]（電話で待つ）

→ 私を待っていてくれてありがとう。　*Thank you for waiting for me.*

→ （電話で）ちょっと待ってください。*Hold on, please*

まつり　**festival** [féstəvəl]

まで（に）　**till** [til], **by** [bai]

→ 5時半まで外で遊んでいいよ。　*You can play outside till five thirty.*

→ 9時までに宿題をおわらせなさい。　*Finish your homework by nine o'clock.*

まど【窓】　**window** [wíndou]

マフラー　**scarf** [skɑ:rf]

ママ　**mom** [mɑm]

まる【丸】　**circle** [sə:rkl]　＝ まわる, わ

まるい【丸い】　**round** [raund]

まわる【回る】　**turn** [tə:rn], **circle** [sə:rkl]

● turn around [əráund] で「ふりむく」の意味になります。

→ 月は地球のまわりを回っています。　*The moon circles the earth.*

マンション　**apartment house** [əpá:rtmənt hàus]

＝ アパート

→ 私はマンションに住んでいます。　*I live in an apartment house.*

まんてん【満点】 **perfect score** [pə́:rfikt skɔːr]

まんなか【真ん中】 **center** [séntər] ＝ちゅうしん

## み ミ

ミカン **orange** [ɔ́:rindʒ] ＝オレンジいろ
● 日本のミカンは mandarin orange と言います。

みぎの【右の】 **right** [rait] ⇔left

みじかい【短い】 **short** [ʃɔːrt] ⇔long

みず【水】 **water** [wɔ́:tər]

みずいろ【水色】 **light blue** [láit blúː]

みずぎ【水着】 **bathing suit** [béiðiŋ sùːt]

みずたまり **puddle** [pʌdl]

みせ **shop** [ʃɑp], **store** [stɔːr]

みせる【見せる】 **show** [ʃou]
➡ あなたのノートを見せて。 *Show me your notebook.*

みち【道】 **road** [roud] ＝どうろ
● でこぼこ道＝bumpy road

みち【道】 **way** [wei] ＝ほうほう, やりかた

みちにまよう【道に迷う】 **be lost** [lɔ(:)st]
➡ 道に迷ってしまった。ここはどこ？ *I'm lost. Where am I?*

みつける【見つける】 **find** [faind] 過去形 found[faund]

ミツバチ **bee** [biː]

みどり【緑】 **green** [griːn]

みなみ【南】 **south** [sauθ]

みにつけている **wear** [weər] ＝きている, かける
➡ 彼女はめがねをかけている。 *She is wearing glasses.*（コンタクトレンズ／くつ／かつら＝contact lenses／shoes／wig）

みにくい **ugly** [ʌ́gli]

みのがす【見逃す】 **overlook** [òuvərlúk]

みぶり【身ぶり】 **gesture** [dʒéstʃər]

みみ【耳】 **ear(s)** [iər(z)]

ミミズ **earthworm** [ə́:rθwə̀:rm]

みやげ **souvenir** [sùːvəníər]

みらい【未来】 **future** [fjúːtʃər] ＝しょうらい

みる【見る】 **look** [luk] ● ～を見る＝look at...
**see** [siː] ＝あう 過去形 saw [sɔː]
**watch** [watʃ] ● テレビを見る＝watch TV
➡ 壁の時計を見てください。 *Please look at the clock on the wall.*

みんな **everyone** [évriwʌn], **everbody** [-badi], **everthing** [-θiŋ], **all** [ɔːl]
➡ みんなつかれていた。 *Everyone was tired.*

## む ム

むこうに **over there** [òuvər ðéər] ＝あちら

むし【虫】 **bug** [bʌg], **insect** [ínsekt], **worm** [wəːrm]
● アリ＝ant [ænt], カ＝mosquito [məskíːtou], カブトムシ＝beetle [bíːtl], カマキリ＝mantis [mæntis], クモ＝spider [spáidər], クワガタムシ＝stag beetle [stæg bíːtl], セミ＝cicada [sikàidə], チョウ＝butterfly [bʌ́tərflài], テントウムシ＝ladybug [léidibʌ̀g], トンボ＝dragonfly [drǽgənflài], バッタ・キリギリス＝grasshopper [grǽshàpər]

むしむしした【蒸し蒸しした】 **humid** [hjúːmid]

むずかしい **difficult** [dífikəlt] ⇔easy 簡単な
**hard** [haːrd] ＝いっしょうけんめい, かたい
➡ 英語を話すのは難しい。 *It is difficult to speak English.*

むすこ【息子】 **son** [sʌn]

むすぶ【結ぶ】 **tie** [tai] ＝ネクタイ

むすめ【娘】 **daughter** [dɔ́ːtər]

むね【胸】 **chest** [tʃest] ＝たんす

むら【村】 **village** [vílidʒ]

むらさきいろ【紫色】 **purple** [pə́:rpl]

むりょうの【無料の】 **free** [friː] ＝ただの, じゆうな, ひまな

## め メ

め【目】 **eye(s)** [ai(z)]
➡ 目を閉じて。 *Close your eyes.*

めい【姪】 **niece** [niːs]

めいれい【命令】 **order** [ɔ́:rdər] ＝ちゅうもん（する）

めいろ【迷路】 **maze** [meiz]

めがね **glasses** [glǽsiz]（必ずsが付きます）

めざましどけい **alarm clock** [əláːrm klàk]
➡ 目覚まし時計を7時にセットしてください。 *Please set the alarm clock for seven o'clock.*

メス **female** [fíːmèil] ● オス＝male [meil]

めずらしい〔珍しい〕 **rare** [reər], **unusual** [ʌnjúːʒuəl]

めだつ〔目立つ〕 **outstanding** [àutstǽndiŋ]

めだまやき〔目玉焼き〕 **fried eggs** [fráid eg]

めったに〜しない **seldom** [séldəm] ＝たまに
→ ぼくはめったにお母さんを手伝いません。 *I seldom help my mother.*

メロン **melon** [mélən]

めをさます **wake up** [weik ʌp] 過去形 woke [wouk] up
→ 起きなさい！7時半よ。 *Wake up! It's seven thirty.*

めんどうくさい〔面倒臭い〕 **troublesome** [trʌ́blsəm]

メンドリ **hen** [hen]

めんるい〔麺類〕 **noodles** [nuːdlz]（必ずsが付きます）

# も　モ

〜も（また） **too** [tuː] ＝あまりにも
→ 私は野球が好きです。弟も好きです。
*I like baseball. My brother likes it, too.*

もういちど〔もう一度〕 **again** [əgén] ＝また

もうひとつの **the other** [ði ʌ́ðər]
→ もう一つの方がほしいです。 *I want the other one.*

もくざい〔木材〕 **wood** [wud]
→ このつくえは木でできている。 *This desk is made of wood.*

もくてき〔目的〕 **aim** [eim], **purpose** [pə́ːrpəs]

もくようび〔木曜日〕 **Thursday** [θə́ːrzdei]

もしも **if** [if]

もじ〔文字〕 **letter** [létər] ＝てがみ

もしもし（電話） **hello** [helóu] ＝こんにちは
→ もしもし。マキです。 *Hello. This is Maki speaking.*

もちろん **of course** [əf kɔ́ːrs], **sure** [ʃuər]

もつ〔持つ〕 **have** [hæv, həv] 過去形 had [hæd, həd]
　　　　 **hold** [hould]（手に持つ） 過去形 held [held]
→ このかばんを持ってください。 *Please hold this bag.*

もっていく〔持って行く〕 **take** [teik] ＝とる, かかる

もっている〔（〜を）持っている〕 **have** [hæv, həv]
＝いる, かう, たべる 過去形 had [hæd, həd]
→ 私は大きな辞書を持っています。 *I have a big dictionary.*

もってくる〔持ってくる〕 **bring** [briŋ] ＝つれてくる

もっと **more** [mɔːr]

もっとよい〔もっと良い〕 **better** [bétər]

もっとわるい〔もっと悪い〕 **worse** [wəːrs]

もどる〔戻る〕 **return** [ritéːrn], **come back** [kʌm bæk]
→ 戻ってきてください！ *Please come back!*

もの〔物〕 **thing** [θiŋ] ＝こと

ものおとをたてる **make (a) noise** [meik (ə) nɔiz]
→ 静かにして！物音をたてないで。 *Be quiet! Do not make any noise.*

モモ **peach** [piːtʃ]

（〜を）もらう **get** [get] 過去形 got [gɑt] ＝うけとる
→ ぼくはおじさんからこの本をもらった。 *I got this book from my uncle.*

もり〔森〕 **forest** [fɔ́ːrist], **woods** [wuz]
→ 森の中に小さな小屋がありました。 *There was a little cottage in the forest.*

もんくをいう〔文句を言う〕 **complain** [kəmpléin]

モンスター **monster** [mɑ́nstər] ＝かいぶつ

もんだい〔問題〕 **problem** [prɑ́bləm]
　　　　 **question** [kwéstʃən] ＝しつもん

# や　ヤ

ヤギ **goat** [gout]

やきゅう〔野球〕 **baseball** [béisbɔ̀ːl]

やきゅうぼう〔野球帽〕 **cap** [kæp] ＝ぼうし

やく〔焼く〕 **bake** [beik], **toast** [toust], **grill** [gril]

やく〔約〕 **about** [əbáut] ● 約20cm＝about 20cm

やくそくする〔約束する〕 **promise** [prɑ́mis]

やくだつ〔役立つ〕 **useful** [júːsfəl]

やさい〔野菜〕 **vegetable** [védʒtəbl]

やさしい **kind** [kaind]
→ 彼女は私にとてもやさしい。 *She is very kind to me*

やすい〔安い〕 **cheap** [tʃiːp] ⇔ expensive

やすみ〔休み〕 **rest** [rest]（休憩）
　　　　 **break** [breik]（ちょっとした短い休み）
　　　　 **vacation** [veikéiʃən]（休暇）
　　　　 **holiday** [hálidei]（休日）
→ ここでひと休みしよう。 *Let's take a break here*

やすんで〔休んで〕 **absent** [ǽbsənt] ＝けっせきの
→ 彼は今日学校を休んでいる。 *He is absent from school today.*

やせる　**lose weight** [luːz weit]

やね【屋根】**roof** [ruːf]

やぶる【破る】**break** [breik]（こわす）

　　　　　**beat** [biːt]（相手を破る，打ち負かす）

　　　　　**tear up** [teər əp]（ひきさく）

➡ 約束を破らないでください。　*Do not break your promise.*

やま【山】**mountain** [máuntin]

やめる　**stop** [stɑp]　＝とまる

➡ おしゃべりをやめてください。　*Please stop talking.*

やりかた【やり方】**way** [wei]，**how to** [hau tə]

やわらかい【柔らかい】**soft** [sɔ(ː)ft]　⇔ **hard** かたい

# ゆ　ユ

ゆ【湯】**hot water** [hát wɔ̀ːtər]

ゆうえんち【遊園地】**amusement** [əmjúːzmənt] **park**

ゆうがた【夕方】**evening** [íːvniŋ]

ゆうかんな【勇敢な】**brave** [breiv]

ゆうしょく【夕食】**dinner** [dínər]，**supper** [sʌ́pər]

ゆうびん【郵便】**mail** [meil]　＝だす

ゆうびんきょく【郵便局】**post office** [póust ɔ̀ːfis]

ゆうびんポスト【郵便ポスト】**mailbox** [méilbɑ̀ks]

ゆうめいな【有名な】**famous** [féiməs]

ユーモア　**humor** [hjúːmər]

ゆうれい【幽霊】**ghost** [goust]　＝おばけ

ゆかいな　**merry** [méri]

ゆき【雪】**snow** [snou]

　◉ 吹雪 ＝ **snow storm** [stɔːrm]

➡ 冬は雪がたくさん降ります。　*We have lots of snow in the winter.*

ゆきのふる【雪の降る】**snowy** [snóui]

ゆっくり　**slowly** [slóuli]

➡ もっとゆっくり話してください。　*Please speak more slowly.*

ゆでる　**boil** [bɔil]　＝にる，わかす

　◉ ゆでたまご ＝ **boiled egg**

➡ なべをわかして卵をゆでなさい。　*Put the pot on the stove and boil an egg.*

ゆび【指】**finger(s)** [fíŋgər(z)]

　◉ 足の指 ＝ **toe** [tou]　◉ つま先 ＝ **tip toe**

ゆるす【許す】**forgive** [fərgív]

　　　　　**excuse** [ikskjúːz]　＝べんかいする

ゆれる【揺れる】**swing** [swiŋ]　過去形 **swung** [swʌŋ]

# よ　ヨ

よい【良い】**good** [gud]　⇔ **bad** 悪い

よういする【用意する】**prepare** [pripéər]　＝じゅんびする

ようこそ　**welcome** [wélkəm]

ようちえん【幼稚園】**kindergarten** [kíndərgàːrtən]

よく　**often** [ɔːfn]　＝たびたび，しょっちゅう

➡ こんなことはよくあることです。　*This often happens.*

よくそう【浴槽】**bathtub** [bǽθtʌb]

よくばりな【欲張りな】**greedy** [gríːdi]

よこ【横】**side** [said]

よこぎって【横切って】**across** [əkrɔ́ːs]

よこになる【横になる】**lie** [lai]　過去形 **lay** [lei]　＝うそ

ヨット　**yacht** [jɑt]

よてい　**plan** [plæn]　＝けいかく（する）

よなか【夜中】**midnight** [mídnait]

よぶ【呼ぶ】**call** [kɔːl]（声を出して呼ぶ）　＝でんわをかける

　　　　　**invite** [inváit]（招待する）

➡ 私をルカと呼んでください。　*Please call me Luka.*

➡ あきこさんも呼ぼうよ。　*Let's invite Akiko, too.*

よふかしする【夜更かしする】**stay up late** [stei ʌp leit]

➡ 夜更かしをしてはいけません。　*Do not stay up late.*

よむ【（〜を）読む】**read** [riːd]　過去形 **read** [red]　※発音注意

　◉ マンガを読む ＝ **read comics**

よやく【予約】**reservation** [rezərvéiʃən]

よやくする【予約する】**reserve** [rizə́ːrv]，**book** [buk]

よる【夜】**night** [nait]

よろしく　**say hello to...**

➡ 君の両親によろしく伝えてください。　*Please say hello to your parents.*

よわい【弱い】**weak** [wiːk]　⇔ **strong** 強い

➡ 今日は元気がでません。　*I feel very weak today.*

# ら　ラ

ライオン　**lion** [láiən]

らいげつ【来月】**next month** [nekst mʌnθ]

やゆよら

らいしゅう【来週】 **next week** [nekst wi:k]

らいねん【来年】 **next year** [nekst jiər]

ラグ **rug** [rʌg]

ラクダ **camel** [kǽməl]

らくな【楽な】 **easy** [íːzi] ＝かんたんな ⇔ difficult

→ 気楽にいこうよ。 *Take it easy.*

ラケット **racket** [rǽkit]

ラッコ **sea otter** [síː ɑtər]

ランプ **lamp** [læmp] ＝でんきスタンド

## り リ

リーダー **leader** [líːdər]

りか【理科】 **science** [sáiəns]

りかいする【(〜を)理解する】 **understand** ＝わかる
[ʌndərstǽnd] 過去形 understood [ʌndərstúd]

→ わかりません。 *I don't understand.*

→ わかりました。 *I understood.*

りきし【力士】 **sumo wrestler** [sumo réslər] ＝すもうとり

りくじょうきょうぎ【陸上競技】 **track** [træk]

りこうな **bright** [brait], **clever** [klévər]

リサイクル **recycle** [rìːsáikl]

りっぱな **excellent** [éksələnt]

りゆう【理由】 **reason** [ríːzən]

りゅうがくする【留学する】 **study abroad** [stʌdi əbɔ̀ːrd]

りょうしん【両親】 **parents** [péərənts]

りょうほう【両方】 **both** [bouθ]

→ ナイフもはさみも両方ともOKですよ。 *Both knives and scissors are OK.*

りょうり【料理】 **cooking** [kúkiŋ]

◉ 料理すること＝cooking ◉ 作った料理＝dish [diʃ]

りょうりする【料理する】 **cook** [kuk] ＝コック

◉ (パンなどを)焼く＝bake [beik], むす, ふかす＝
steam [stiːm], (油で)焼く, いためる＝fry [frai],
(焼き網で)焼く, あぶる＝grill [gril], わかす, 煮る,
ゆでる＝boil [bɔil], とろ火で煮る＝stew [stjuː]

→ ぼくのおじいさんが夕食を作りました。
*My grandfather cooked dinner.*

りょうりにん【料理人】 **cook** [kuk] ＝コック, りょうりする

りょくちゃ【緑茶】 **green tea** [gríːn tìː]

りょこうをする【旅行をする】 **travel** [trǽvəl] ＝たび

**go on a trip** [trip]

過去形 went on a trip

→ 私達は北海道へ旅行に行きました。 *We went on a trip to Hokkaido.*

リンゴ **apple** [ǽpl]

## る ル

るすにする【留守にする】 **be out** ＝がいしゅつしている

るすばんでんわ【留守番電話】 **answering machine**
[ǽnsəriŋ məʃíːn]

→ 留守番電話にメッセージを残しておいてください。
*Please leave a message on my answering machine.*

## れ レ

れい【例】 **example** [igzǽmpl]

◉ 例えば＝for example

れい【礼】 **bow** [bau] (＝おじぎ)

れいぎただしい【礼儀正しい】 **polite** [pəláit]

→ 彼女はいつもみんなに礼儀正しくてやさしい。 *She is always polite and friendly to everyone.*

れいぞうこ【冷蔵庫】 **fridge** [fridʒ]
＝ refrigerator [rifrídʒərèitər]

→ 冷蔵庫の扉を開けっ放しにしないで。 *Don't leave the fridge door open.*

れいぼう【冷房】 **air conditioner** [kəndíʃənər]

レインコート **raincoat** [réinkòut]

レース **race** [reis]

レジがかり【レジ係】 **cashier** [kæʃiər]

レストラン **restaurant** [réstərənt]

レタス **lettuce** [létis]

れつ【列】 **line** [lain], **row** [rou]

れつにならぶ【列に並ぶ】 **get in line** [gét in làin]
過去形 got in line [gát in làin]

→ 全員整列。列に入りなさい! *Line up, everyone. Get in line!*

レディ **lady** [léidi] ＝おんなのひと

レモン **lemon** [lémən]

レンジ **stove** [stouv] (料理用のガスこんろ) ＝ガスレン

oven [ʌ́vən]（電子レンジ）＝オーブン

● 正式には microwave[máikrəwèiv] oven

**れんしゅうする**〖練習する〗 **practice** [prǽktis]

＝けいこする

→ 今晩ピアノの練習をしなければいけません。 *I have to practice the piano tonight.*

## ろ ロ

**ろうか**〖廊下〗 **hall way** [hɔ́ːl wèi]

→ ろうかを走ってはいけません。 *Don't run in the hall way.*

**ろうそく candle** [kǽndl]

**ローラースケート roller skating** [róulərskèitiŋ]

**ろくおんする**〖録音する〗 **record** [rikɔ́ːrd]

**ろくがつ**〖6月〗 **June** [dʒuːn]

**ロケット rocket** [rákit]

**ロバ donkey** [dáŋki]

**ロボット robot** [róubət]

## わ ワ

**わ**〖輪〗 **circle** [sə́ːrkl] ＝まる，まわる

→ 大きな輪を作ろう。 *Let's make a big circle.*

**ワイン wine** [wain]

→ ワインはブドウから作られます。 *Wine is made from grapes.*

**わかい**〖若い〗 **young** [jʌŋ] ⇔old としとった

→ 若く見えますね。 *You look young.*

**わかす boil** [bɔil] ＝にる，ゆでる，ふっとうする

**わがままな selfish** [sélfiʃ]

→ 彼はわがままだ。 *He is selfish.*

**わかる understand** [ʌ̀ndərstǽnd] ＝りかいする

**know** [nou] ＝しっている

→ わかってるよ! *I know!*

**わかれる part** [pɑːrt]

**わくせい**〖惑星〗 **planet** [plǽnit]

**わける**〖分ける〗 **share** [ʃéər]

**わざと on purpose** [pə́ːrpəs]

→ 彼はわざとグラスを割った。 *He broke the glass on purpose.*

**ワシ eagle** [íːgl]

**わすれる forget** [fərgét] 過去形 forgot [fərgát]

**leave** [liːv]（置き忘れる） 過去形 left [left]

→ 忘れました。 *I forgot.*

→ 私は学校にかばんを忘れた。 *I left my bag at school.*

**わたしたちの**〖私達の〗 **our** [áuər] ＝ぼくたちの

→ 私達の担任は山田先生です。 *Our homeroom teacher is Mr. Yamada.*

**わたしたちは（が）**〖私達は（が）〗 **we** [wiː, wi]

＝ぼくたちは（が）

→ 私達はいい友達です。 *We are good friends.*

**わたしたちを（に）**〖私達を（に）〗 **us** [ʌs, əs]

＝ぼくたちを（に）

**わたしの**〖私の〗 **my** [mai] ＝ぼくの

→ 私の名前は愛子です。 *My name is Aiko.*

**わたしは（が）**〖私は（が）〗 **I** [ai] ＝ぼくは（が）

→ 私は学生です。 *I'm a student.*

**わたしを（に）**〖私を（に）〗 **me** [miː] ＝ぼくを（に）

→ 私に本を見せてください。 *Please show me your book.*

**わたす**〖渡す〗 **hand** [hænd] ＝くばる， **pass** [pæs]

→ 塩を取ってください（私に手渡してください）。

*Pass me the salt, please.*

**わたる**〖渡る〗 **cross** [krɔ(ː)s] ＝こうさする

→ 通りを渡る時は気をつけて。 *Be careful when you cross the street.*

**ワニ alligator** [ǽləgèitər]， **crocodile** [krákədàil]

● alligator（アメリカなど），crocodile（アフリカなど）

**わらう**〖笑う〗 **laugh** [læf]（声を出して笑う）

**smile** [smail]（にっこり笑う） ＝ほほえむ

→ 私を笑わないでください。 *Don't laugh at me.*

**わりざんをする**〖割り算をする〗 **divide** [diváid]

→ 10÷2＝5 *Ten divided by two is (makes) five.*

**わるい**〖悪い〗 **bad** [bæd] ⇔good 良い

**わん**〖湾〗 **bay** [bei]

れ
ろ
わ

31

# English ▼ Japanese

## 英和辞書
English-Japanese Dictionary

### 見出し語

見出し語は、子供達の身近な語1,400語を選び、基本語彙564語については太字で示し、それ以外の語彙は細字で示しました。動詞の過去形については、不規則動詞の過去形および study ⇒ studied のような変化の語彙のみ、示しました。

かずと世界の主要な国名については紙面の都合上別表にして本文の最後のページに掲げました。

The English-Japanese Dictionary contains 1,400 words. 564 basic words from the first section are indicated in bold. Only the past tense of irregular verbs are shown because of limited space available. Lists of numbers and major countries in the world are provided at the end of this book.

### 品詞略語一覧

| | | |
|---|---|---|
| 名…名詞 | 副…副詞 | 代…代名詞 |
| 動…動詞 | 助…助動詞 | 接…接続詞 |
| 形…形容詞 | 前…前置詞 | 間…間投詞 |

## A a [ei]

about [əbáut] 副 約, およそ　前 ～について

abroad [əbrɔ́:d] 副 外国へ, 海外に

absent [ǽbsənt] 形 休んで, 欠席の

accident [ǽksədənt] 名 事故, 災難

across [əkrɔ́:s] 副 横切って

address [ǽdres, ədrés] 名 あて先, 住所

advise [ədváiz] 動 ～に忠告する, ～を勧める

afraid [əfréid] 形 こわがって, おそれて
 ● be afraid of... ～をこわがる

after [ǽftər] 前 ～の後に
 ● after school 放課後

afternoon [ǽftərnú:n] 名 昼, 午後
 ● Good afternoon. こんにちは。

again [əgén] 副 また, もう一度

ago [əgóu] 副 ～前に

agree [əgrí:] 動 賛成する, 同意する

aim [eim] 名 目的

air [eər] 名 空気, 空　● air conditioner [kəndíʃənər] 冷房

airplane [éərplèin] 名 飛行機

airport [éərpɔ̀:rt] 名 空港

alarm clock [əlá:rm klàk] 名 めざまし時計

album [ǽlbəm] 名 アルバム

alive [əláiv] 形 生きて

all [ɔ:l] 形 すべての　名 すべて

alligator [ǽləgèitər] 名 ワニ (アメリカや中国産など)

almost [ɔ́:lmoust] 副 ほとんど

alone [əlóun] 副 ひとりで, 単独で

alphabet [ǽlfəbèt] 名 アルファベット

always [ɔ́:lwiz] 副 いつも, つねに

ambulance [ǽmbjuləns] 名 救急車

angry [ǽŋgri] 形 怒った

animal [ǽnəməl] 名 動物

another [ənʌ́ðər] 形 別の, もうひとつの
 ● one after another 次々と

answer [ǽnsər] 動 答える　名 返事

ant [ænt] 名 アリ

any [éni] 形 いくつかの, どれでも, (否定文で)少しも～ない

apartment house [əpá:rtmənt hàus] 名 アパート, マンション

apple [ǽpl] 名 リンゴ

apple pie [pai] 名 アップルパイ

April [éiprəl] 名 4月

aquarium [əkwéəriəm] 名 水族館

arm(s) [a:rm(z)] 名 うで, 武器

armchair [á:rmtʃèər] 名 ひじかけいす

arrive [əráiv] 動 到着する, 着く
 ● arrive at... ～に到着する

arts and crafts [á:rts ənd kræfts] 名 図工

ask [æsk] 動 (～を)たずねる, 聞く, たのむ

astronaut [ǽstrənɔ̀:t] 名 宇宙飛行士

ate [eit] 動 食べた　eatの過去形

atlas [ǽtləs] 名 地図

August [ɔ́:gəst] 名 8月

aunt [ænt] 名 おば

## B b [bi:]

back [bæk] 形 後ろの　名 背中

bacon [béikən] 名 ベーコン

bad [bæd] 形 悪い ⇔ good 良い

badminton [bǽdmintən] 名 バドミントン

bag [bæg] 名 かばん

bake [beik] 動 焼く (パンやケーキなど)

bakery [béikəri] 名 パン屋

banana [bənǽnə] 名 バナナ

bank [bæŋk] 名 銀行

bar [ba:r] 名 棒　● monkey bars うんてい

barbecue [bá:rbəkjù:] 名 バーベキュー

bark [ba:rk] 動 ほえる

baseball [béisbɔ̀:l] 名 野球

basket [bǽskit] 名 かご

basketball [bǽskitbɔ̀:l] 名 バスケットボール

bat [bæt] 名 コウモリ

bathing suit [béiðiŋ sjù:t] 名 水着

bathroom [bǽθrù:m] 名 浴室, お手洗い

bathtub [bǽθtʌ̀b] 名 浴槽 (よくそう)

bear [beər] 名 クマ　動 生む　過去形 bore [bɔ:r]

beat [bi:t] 動 (～を)打つ, 負かす　過去形 beat [bi:t] (同形)

beautiful [bjú:təfəl] 形 美しい

became [bikéim] 動 ～になった　becomeの過去形

because [bikɔ́:z] 接 だから, なぜならば

become [bikʌ́m] 動 ～になる　過去形 became [bikéim]

bed [bed] 名 ベッド

bedroom [bédrù:m] 名 寝室

bee [bi:] 名 ミツバチ

beer [biər] 名 ビール

before [bifɔ́:r] 前 ～の前に(を)

be from [bi: frəm] ～出身である

began [bigǽn] 動 (～を)始めた, 始まった　beginの過去形

begin [bigín] 動 (～を)始める, 始まる　過去形 began [bigǽn]

bell [bel] 名 鈴, ベル, 鐘

belly [béli] 名 おなか

**B**
**C**

bellybutton [bélibÀtən] 名 おへそ

bench [bentʃ] 名 ベンチ

best [best] 形 いちばん良い

**between** [bitwíːn] 前 ～の間に

**bicycle** [báisikl] 名 自転車

**big** [big] 形 大きい

**bike** [baik] 名 自転車 = **bicycle**, オートバイ

**bird** [bəːrd] 名 鳥

birthday [báːrθdèi] 名 誕生日

bit [bit] 動 噛んだ(かんだ)  bite の過去形

bite [bait] 動 噛む(かむ) 過去形 bit [bit]

**black** [blæk] 名 黒

**blackboard** [blǽkbɔ̀ːrd] 名 黒板

blew [bluː] 動 吹いた  blow の過去形

blood [blʌd] 名 血

**blouse** [blaus] 名 ブラウス

blow [blou] 動 吹く 過去形 blew [bluː]

**blue** [bluː] 名 青  ● *light blue* [lait] 水色

**blueberry** [blúːbèri] 名 ブルーベリー

**boat** [bout] 名 ボート

body [bádi] 名 身体  ● *body parts* [paːrts] 身体の部分

boil [bɔil] 動 わかす, にる, ゆでる

 ● *boiled egg* ゆで卵

**book** [buk] 名 本 動 予約する

bore [bɔːr] 動 うんざりさせる, いやにさせる

**boring** [bɔ́ːriŋ] 形 退屈な

borrow [bárou] 動 借りる

both [bouθ] 副 両方, どちらも

bottle [batl] 名 ボトル

 ● *plastic bottle* ペットボトル

bottom [bátəm] 名 底 形 底の, 最下部の

**bought** [bɔːt] 動 (～を)買った  buy の過去形

bow [bau] 名 礼, おじぎ 動 おじぎする

bowling [bóuliŋ] 名 ボウリング

box [baks] 名 箱

boy [bɔi] 名 男の子, 男子

**brave** [breiv] 形 勇敢な(ゆうかんな)

**bread** [bred] 名 パン

**break** [breik] 動 (～を)こわす, やぶる 過去形 broke [brouk]
 名 休憩, 休み

breakfast [brékfəst] 名 朝ごはん, 朝食

bridge [bridʒ] 名 橋

bright [brait] 形 明るい, 頭が良い, 利口な

bring [briŋ] 動 連れてくる, 持ってくる 過去形 brought [brɔːt]

**broccoli** [brákəli] 名 ブロッコリー

**broke** [brouk] 動 (～を)こわした, やぶれた  break の過去形

brother [brʌ́ðər] 名 兄弟

 ● *big brother* 兄   ● *little brother* 弟

brought [brɔːt] 動 連れてきた, 持ってきた  bring の過去形

**brown** [braun] 名 茶色

brush [brʌʃ] 名 はけ, ブラシ

bubble [bʌbl] 名 泡, シャボン玉

bug [bʌg] 名 虫, 昆虫

build [bild] 動 (～を)建てる, (～を)作る 過去形 built [bilt]

building [bíldiŋ] 名 建物, ビルディング

built [bilt] 動 (～を)建てた, (～を)作った  build の過去形

**bullet train** [búlit trein] 名 新幹線

bump [bʌmp] 動 ぶつける 名 こぶ

**bus** [bʌs] 名 バス  ● *bus stop* バス停

businessman [bíznismæn] 名 会社員, 実業家

**busy** [bízi] 形 いそがしい

but [bʌt, bət] 接 でも, しかし

button [bʌ́tən] 名 ボタン

**buy** [bai] 動 (～を)買う 過去形 bought [bɔːt]

 ● *buy groceries* [gróusəriz] 食料品を買う

**by** [bai] 前 ～のそばに, ～までに

# C c [siː]

**cabbage** [kǽbidʒ] 名 キャベツ

**cake** [keik] 名 ケーキ

calendar [kǽləndər] 名 カレンダー

call [kɔːl] 動 (～を)呼ぶ, 電話をかける

**came** [keim] 動 来た  come の過去形

camel [kǽməl] 名 ラクダ

camera [kǽmərə] 名 カメラ

**can** [kæn, kən] 助 ～できる 過去形 could [kud, kəd] 名 缶

candle [kǽndl] 名 ろうそく

**cap** [kæp] 名 帽子, 野球帽

capital [kǽpitəl] 名 首都

**car** [kɑːr] 名 自動車

careful [kéərfəl] 形 注意深い, しんちょうな

**carefully** [kéərfəli] 副 注意深く

carried [kǽrid] 動 (～を)運んだ  carry の過去形

**carrot** [kǽrət] 名 にんじん

carry [kǽri] 動 (～を)運ぶ 過去形 carried [kǽrid]

**cat** [kæt] 名 ネコ

**catch** [kætʃ] 動 (～を)つかまえる 過去形 caught [kɔːt]

caterpillar [kǽtərpilər] 名 毛虫, イモムシ

**caught** [kɔːt] 動 (～を)つかまえた  catch の過去形

ceiling [síːliŋ] 名 天井

 ● *ceiling light* [lait] 天井の電気

center [séntər] 名 真ん中, 中心

century [séntʃəri] 名 世紀

● *the 20th century* [twéntiiθ] 20世紀

ceremony [sérəmòuni] 名 式

  ● *opening ceremony* [óupəniŋ] 始業式

  ● *closing ceremony* [klóuziŋ] 終業式

**chair** [tʃeər] 名 いす

**chalk** [tʃɔ:k] 名 チョーク

**chance** [tʃæns] 名 (幸運な)機会, 偶然　形 偶然の, はずみの

**change** [tʃeindʒ] 動 (～を)変える　名 変化, つりせん

**cheap** [tʃl:p] 形 安い ⇔ expensive 高い

cheat [tʃi:t] 動 だます, カンニングをする

chest [tʃest] 名 胸, 整理ダンス

chick [tʃik] 名 ヒヨコ

**child** [tʃaild] 名 子ども　複数形 children

**children** [tʃíldrən] 名 子どもたち　childの複数形

chimney [tʃímni] 名 えんとつ

chin [tʃin] 名 あご

choose [tʃu:z] 動 ～を選ぶ　過去形 chose [tʃouz]

church [tʃə:rtʃ] 名 (キリスト教の)教会

circle [sə:rkl] 名 丸, 輪　動 輪を作る, ～の周りをまわる

**city hall** [síti hɔːl] 名 市役所

clap [klæp] 動 手をたたく　過去形 clapped [klæpt]

class [klæs] 名 クラス, 授業

**classroom** [klǽsrù:m] 名 教室

clean [kli:n] 動 (～を)そうじする, きれいにする

  ● *clean the toilet* [tɔ́ilit]　トイレをそうじする

clean [kli:n] 形 きれいな, 清潔な ⇔ dirty よごれた

cleaning [klí:niŋ] 名 そうじ

clever [klévər] 形 利口な, かしこい

click [klik] 動 クリックする, カチッと音がする

climb [klaim] 動 (～に)登る　● *climb a tree* 木に登る

clock [klɑk] 名 時計 (置時計, 掛け時計)

close [klouz] 動 (～を)閉める

close [klous] 形 近い

closet [klázit] 名 戸だな, 押入れ

clothes [klouz] 名 服

**cloud** [klaud] 名 雲

**cloudy** [kláudi] 形 (天気)曇りの

club [klʌb] 名 クラブ, クラブのふだ(トランプ)

  ● *club activities* [æktívətiz]　クラブ活動

**coffee** [kɔ́(:)fi] 名 コーヒー

coin [kɔin] 名 コイン, 硬貨

cola [kóulə] 名 コーラ (Coca-Cola コカコーラのこと)

**cold** [kould] 形 寒い ⇔ hot 暑い

collect [kəlékt] 動 集める, 収集する

college [kálidʒ] 名 大学, 専門学校

color [kálər] 名 色　動 色をぬる

**come** [kʌm] 動 来る　過去形 came [keim]

comics [kámiks] 名 マンガ

comfortable [kʌ́mfərtəbl] 形 気持ちのよい, くつろいだ

common [kámən] 形 共通の, ふつうの

  ● *common sense* [sens] 常識

company [kʌ́mpəni] 名 会社, 仲間

complain [kəmpléin] 動 文句を言う, 不平を言う

**computer** [kəmpjú:tər] 名 コンピューター

continue [kəntínju:] 動 続く, 継続(けいぞく)する

convenient [kənví:njənt] 形 便利な, 使いやすい

**cook** [kuk] 動 (～を)料理する　名 コック, 料理人

  ● *cook dinner* [dínər]　夕食をつくる

cookie [kúki] 名 クッキー

cooking [kúkiŋ] 名 料理, 料理をすること

**cool** [ku:l] 形 すずしい

**corn** [kɔ:rn] 名 とうもろこし

could [kud, kəd] 助 ～できた　canの過去形

Could you...?　～してもらえますか?

count [kaunt] 動 (～を)数える

couple [kʌpl] 名 2つ, 夫婦　● *a couple of...* 2つの～

course [kɔ:rs] 名 コース, なりゆき　● *of course* もちろん

**cousin** [kʌ́zən] 名 いとこ

**cow** [kau] 名 ウシ (雌牛: めうし)

**cried** [kraid] 動 叫んだ, 泣いた　cryの過去形

criminal [krímənəl] 名 犯人　形 犯罪の, 罪になる

crocodile [krákədàil] 名 ワニ (アフリカ産など)

cross [krɔ(:)s] 動 渡る, 交差する

**cry** [krai] 動 叫ぶ, 泣く　過去形 cried [kraid]

**cucumber** [kjú:kəmbər] 名 きゅうり

**curtain** [kə:rtn] 名 カーテン

**cut** [kʌt] 動 (～を)切る　過去形 cut [kʌt] (同形)

cute [kju:t] 形 かわいい

# D d [di:]

dad [dæd] 名 パパ

**dance** [dæns] 動 おどる

danger [déindʒər] 名 危険

dangerous [déindʒərəs] 形 危険な, 危ない

**dark** [da:rk] 形 暗い ⇔ light 明るい

date [deit] 名 日付

daughter [dɔ́:tər] 名 娘 (むすめ)

**day** [dei] 名 日, 1日　● *one day* 1日

dead [ded] 形 死んだ, 死んでいる

dear [diər] 形 親愛なる, ～様 (手紙の書き出しはDear)

death [deθ] 名 死, 終わり

**December** [disémbər] 名 12月

decide [disáid] 動 決める

**D**
**E**

deep [di:p] 形 深い

delicious [dilíʃəs] 形 とてもおいしい

**dentist** [déntist] 名 歯医者

**department store** [dipá:rtmənt stɔ̀:r] 名 デパート

**desk** [desk] 名 机

dessert [dizə́:rt] 名 デザート

diary [dáiəri] 名 日記

**dictionary** [díkʃənèri] 名 辞書

die [dai] 動 死ぬ 過去形 died [daid]

different [dífərənt] 形 ちがった, 別の, いろいろの

**difficult** [dífikəlt] 形 むずかしい ⇔ easy 簡単な

dig [dig] 動 (～を)ほる 過去形 dug [dʌg]

dining room [dáiniŋ ru:m] 食堂, ダイニングルーム

dinner [dínər] 名 夕食, 夕飯

**dinosaur** [dáinəsɔ̀:r] 名 恐竜(きょうりゅう)

direction [dirékʃn] 名 方向, 命令, 指示

**dirty** [də́:rti] 形 きたない ⇔ clean きれいな

discover [diskʌ́vər] 動 (～を)発見する, (～に)気づく

discuss [diskʌ́s] 動 話し合う, (～を)論じ合う

dish [diʃ] 名 皿, 料理(作った料理のことをいう)

divide [diváid] 動 ～を分ける, 割り算をする

**doctor** [dáktər] 名 医者

**dodgeball** [dádʒbɔ̀:l] 名 ドッジボール

**dog** [dɔ:g] 名 イヌ

doll [dɑl] 名 人形

dollar [dálər] 名 ドル($)

donkey [dáŋki] 名 ロバ

**door** [dɔ:r] 名 ドア

dragonfly [drǽgənflài] 名 トンボ

**drank** [dræŋk] 動 飲んだ drinkの過去形

**draw** [drɔ:] 動 (～を)えがく, かく 過去形 drew [dru:]

dream [dri:m] 名 夢

dress [dres] 名 ドレス

**drew** [dru:] 動 (～を)えがいた, かいた drawの過去形

**drink** [driŋk] 動 (～を)飲む 過去形 drank [dræŋk]

**drive** [draiv] 動 (～を)運転する 過去形 drove [drouv]

drop [drɑp] 名 しずく 動 (ぽたぽた)落ちる 過去形 dropped

dropped [drɑpt] 動 (ぽたぽた)落ちた dropの過去形

**drove** [drouv] 動 (～を)運転した driveの過去形

dry [drai] 形 乾いた 動 (～を)乾かす, 干す 過去形 dried [draid]

**duck** [dʌk] 名 アヒル

dug [dʌg] 動 (～を)ほった digの過去形

during [djú(:)əriŋ] 前 ～じゅう, ～のあいだじゅう

dust [dʌst] 名 ほこり

## E e [i:]

each [i:tʃ] 形 それぞれの

eagle [i:gl] 名 ワシ

**ear(s)** [iər] 名 耳

**early** [ə́:rli] 副 早く

earth [ə:rθ] 名 地球(the earth)

**earthquake** [ə́:rθkwèik] 名 地震

earthworm [ə́:rθwə̀:rm] 名 ミミズ

**easy** [í:zi] 形 かんたんな ⇔ difficult むずかしい

**eat** [i:t] 動 (～を)食べる 過去形 ate [eit]

effort [éfərt] 名 努力

　　● *make an effort* 努力する

egg [eg] 名 卵

**eighth** [eiθ] 形 8番目の(the eighth)

electric [iléktrik] 形 電気の, 電動の

**elementary school** [èləméntəri sku:l] 名 小学校

**elephant** [éləfənt] 名 ゾウ

elevator [éləvèitər] 名 エレベーター

**eleventh** [ilévənθ] 形 11番目の(the eleventh)

e-mail [í:meil] 名 eメール

empty [émpti] 形 からの, 中身のない 動 (～を)からにする
　　過去形 emptied [émptied]

encourage [inkə́:ridʒ] 動 はげます, 勇気づける

end [end] 名 端, 最後, 終わり

**English** [íŋgliʃ] 名 英語

**enjoy** [indʒɔ́i] 動 (～を)楽しむ

enough [inʌ́f] 形 十分な, 足りる

entrance [éntrəns] 名 入口, 入学

　　● *entrance ceremony* 入学式

**eraser** [iréisər] 名 消しゴム, 黒板消し

escalator [éskəlèitər] 名 エスカレーター

**evening** [í:vniŋ] 名 夕方

　　● *Good evening.* こんばんは。

every [évri] 形 毎～, どの～も, ～ごと

　　● *every day* 毎日

everybody [évribàdi] 代 だれでも, みんな

everyday [évridèi] 形 毎日の, 普段の

everyone [évriwʌ̀n] 代 みんな, だれでも

everything [évriθìŋ] 代 すべて, すべてのこと(もの)

examination [igzæmənéiʃən] 名 試験

example [igzǽmpl] 名 例 ● *for example* 例えば

excellent [éksələnt] 形 りっぱな, 優秀な

excited [iksáitid] 形 興奮した, 活気のある

exciting [iksáitiŋ] 形 興奮させる, はらはらさせる

excuse [ikskjú:s] 名 弁解

excuse [ikskjú:z] 動 弁解する

　　● *Excuse me...* 失礼ですが…

exercise [éksərsàiz] 動 運動する 名 運動, 訓練

exit [éɡzit] 名 出口

expensive [ikspénsiv] 形 (値段が)高い

explain [ikspléin] 動 (〜を)説明する

express [iksprés] 動 (〜を)表現する　名 速達便　形 急行の

eye(s) [ái(z)] 名 目

# F f [ef]

face [feis] 名 顔

fail [feil] 動 失敗する, (試験などに)落ちる

fall [fɔːl] 動 落ちる　過去形 fell [fel]　名 秋

family [fǽməli] 名 家族

famous [féiməs] 形 有名な

farm [fɑːrm] 名 農場

farmer [fáːrmər] 名 農夫

farming [fáːrmiŋ] 名 農業

fast [fæst] 形 速い ⇔ slow 遅い

fat [fæt] 形 太った ⇔ thin やせた

father [fáːðər] 名 お父さん, 父

feather [féðər] 名 羽毛

February [fébruəri] 名 2月

fed [fed] 動 えさを与えた　feedの過去形

feed [fiːd] 動 (動物に)えさを与える, (家族を)養う 過去形 fed [fed]
　　● *feed the pet* ペットにえさを与える

feel [fiːl] 動 感じる　過去形 felt [felt]

feet [fiːt] 名 あし(足首からつま先)　footの複数形

fell [fel] 動 落ちた　fallの過去形

felt [felt] 動 感じた　feelの過去形

female [fíːmeil] 名 女性, (動物の)メス

ferry [féri] 名 フェリー

festival [féstəvəl] 名 祭り

fever [fíːvər] 名 熱

few [fjuː] 形 少ししかない　● *a few* 2, 3の, 少しの

field trip [fíːld trìp] 名 遠足

fifth [fifθ] 形 5番目の (the fifth)

fight [fait] 名 けんか　動 戦う 過去形 fought [fɔːt]

find [faind] 動 (〜を)見つける 過去形 found [faund]

fine [fain] 形 (天気)晴れた, 元気な

finger(s) [fíŋɡər(z)] 名 指

finish [fíniʃ] 動 終わる, (〜を)終える

fire [fáiər] 名 火, 炎　● *firefighter* [faitər] 消防士
　　● *fire engine* [éndʒin] 消防車
　　● *fire station* [stéiʃən] 消防署

fireworks [fáiərwə̀ːrks] 名 花火

first [fəːrst] 形 最初の, 1番目の (the first)
　　● *first of all* まずはじめに

fish [fiʃ] 名 魚 単複同形 fish

fix [fiks] 動 固定する, 直す

flag [flæɡ] 名 旗

flew [fluː] 動 飛んだ　flyの過去形

flight attendant [flait əténdənt] 名 航空機の客室乗務員

florist [flɔ́(ː)rist] 名 花屋さん, 花屋(職業)

flower [fláuər] 名 花　● *flower bed* 花だん

fly [flai] 動 飛ぶ 過去形 flew [fluː]

food [fuːd] 名 食べ物, 食料

fool [fuːl] 名 ばかもの, おろかもの

foolish [fúːliʃ] 形 おろかな, ばかな

foot [fut] 名 あし(足首からつま先)　複数形 feet [fiːt]

football [fútbɔ̀ːl] 名 アメリカンフットボール　● イギリスでは
　　soccer のことを言う。

forehead [fɔ́(ː)rid] 名 ひたい

foreign [fɔ́ːrin] 形 外国の, 外国産の
　　● *foreign language* [lǽŋɡwidʒ] 外国語

forest [fɔ́(ː)rist] 名 森

forgave [fərɡéiv] 動 (〜を)ゆるした　forgiveの過去形

forget [fərɡét] 動 (〜を)忘れる 過去形 forgot [fərɡát]

forgive [fərɡív] 動 (〜を)ゆるす 過去形 forgave [fərɡéiv]

forgot [fərɡát] 動 (〜を)忘れた　forgetの過去形

fork [fɔːrk] 名 フォーク

fought [fɔːt] 動 戦った　fightの過去形

found [faund] 動 (〜を)見つけた　findの過去形

fountain [fáuntən] 名 泉, 噴水

fourth [fɔːrθ] 形 4番目の (the fourth)

fox [fɑks] 名 キツネ

free [friː] 形 無料の, ただの, 自由な

French fries [fréntʃ fràiz] 名 ポテトフライ

Friday [fráidei] 名 金曜日

fridge [fridʒ] 名 冷蔵庫 ＝refrigerator

fried [fraid] 動 (油で)焼いた, いためた　fryの過去形

fried chicken [fraid tʃíkin] 名 フライドチキン

friend [frend] 名 友だち

fruit [fruːt] 名 果物

fry [frai] 動 (油で)焼く, いためる 過去形 fried [fraid]

full [ful] 形 いっぱいの ⇔ empty からの

fun [fʌn] 名 おもしろみ, 楽しみ

funny [fʌ́ni] 形 おかしな, こっけいな

future [fjúːtʃər] 名 未来, 将来

# G g [dʒiː]

game [ɡeim] 名 試合, ゲーム

garage [ɡərɑ́ːdʒ] 名 ガレージ

garden [ɡáːrdən] 名 庭

gave [ɡeiv] 動 (〜を)与えた　giveの過去形

**geese** [gi:s] 名 ガチョウ　gooseの複数形

**gesture** [dʒéstʃər] 名 身ぶり, ジェスチャー

**get** [get] 動 （～を）もらう, 受け取る　過去形 got [gɑt]

**get in line** [lain]　列にならぶ

**get lost** [lɔ:st, lɔst]　道にまよう

**get off...**　～から降りる

　　● *get off the train*　電車から降りる

**get on...**　～に乗る　● *get on the train*　電車に乗る

**get to...**　～に到着する

**get up**　起きる

**ghost** [goust] 名 おばけ, ゆうれい

**giraffe** [dʒəráf] 名 キリン

**girl** [gə:rl] 名 女の子, 女子

**give** [giv] 動 （～を）与える, くれる　過去形 gave [geiv]

**glad** [glæd] 形 うれしい

**glass** [glæs] 名 コップ, ガラス

**glasses** [glǽsiz] 名 めがね

**globe** [gloub] 名 地球儀, 地球

**glue** [glu:] 名 のり　動 くっつける

**go** [gou] 動 行く　過去形 went [went]

**go away** [əwéi]　去る

**go camping** [kǽmpiŋ]　キャンプに行く

**go on a trip** [trip]　旅行をする

**go shopping** [ʃápiŋ]　買い物に行く

**go to bed** [bed]　寝る, 床につく

**goat** [gout] 名 ヤギ

**gold** [gould] 名 金色

**golf** [gɑlf] 名 ゴルフ

**good** [gud] 形 良い ⇔ bad 悪い

　　● *be good at...*　（～が）得意である

**goodbye** [gùdbái] 間 さようなら

**goose** [gu:s] 名 ガチョウ　複数形 geese [gi:s]

**got** [gɑt] 動 （～を）もらった, 受け取った　getの過去形

**grade** [greid] 名 成績, 学年

**graduation** [grædʒuéiʃən] 名 卒業

　　● *graduate* [grædʒuit]　卒業生

　　● *graduation ceremony* [sérəmouni]　卒業式

**grandchild** [grǽndtʃàild] 名 孫　複数形 grandchildren

**grandfather** [grǽndfɑ̀:ðər] 名 おじいさん, 祖父

**grandmother** [grǽndmʌ̀ðər] 名 おばあさん, 祖母

**grapefruit** [gréipfrù:t] 名 グレープフルーツ

**grapes** [greips] 名 ブドウ（通常sを付けてgrapes）

**grass** [græs] 名 草

**grasshopper** [grǽshàpər] 名 バッタ

**gray** [grei] 名 グレー

**greedy** [grí:di] 形 食いしんぼうな, よくばりな

**green** [gri:n] 名 緑色

**green pepper** [pépər]　ピーマン

**green tea** [ti:]　緑茶

grew [gru:] 動 育てた, 成長した　growの過去形

grill [gril] 名 （肉や魚の）焼き網　動 （肉や魚などを）焼く, あぶ

group [gru:p] 名 グループ

grow [grou] 動 成長する, 育てる　過去形 grew [gru:]

guess [ges] 動 （～と）推測する, 思う, 言い当てる

guest [gest] 名 客

guitar [gitá:r] 名 ギター

**gym** [dʒim] 名 体育館

**gymnastics** [dʒimnǽstiks] 名 きかい体操

# H h [eitʃ]

**had** [hæd, həd] 動 （～を）持っていた, （～を）食べた,
　（家族や友達が）いた, ペットを飼っていた　haveの過去形

hair [héər] 名 髪

hairbrush [héərbrʌ̀ʃ] 名 ヘアブラシ　● *comb* [koum]　くし

half [hæf, hɑ:f] 形 名 半分（の）, 半分のもの

hall [hɔ:l] 名 ホール, 玄関

hallway [hɔ́:lwèi] 名 ろうか

**hamburger** [hǽmbə̀:rgər] 名 ハンバーガー

**hand(s)** [hænd(z)] 名 手　動 渡す, 配る, 提出する

handkerchief [hǽŋkərtʃi(:)f] 名 ハンカチ

handsome [hǽnsəm] 形 ハンサムな, 顔立ちが美しい

hang [hæŋ] 動 つるす, ぶらさがる, かける　過去形 hung [hʌŋ]

happen [hǽpən] 動 起こる

**happy** [hǽpi] 形 うれしい

**hard** [hɑ:rd] 副 一生けん命に　形 かたい ⇔ soft やわらかい
　形 むずかしい ⇔ easy 簡単な

**hat** [hæt] 名 帽子（ふちあり）

hate [heit] 動 きらう, にくむ

**have** [hæv, həv] 動 （～を）持っている, （～を）食べる,
　（家族や友達が）いる, ペットを飼う　過去形 had [hæd, həd]

　　● *have breakfast* [brékfəst]　朝食をとる

**have a good time**　楽しい時を過ごす

**have to**　～しなければならない

**he** [hi:] 代 彼は, 彼が

head [hed] 名 頭

headache [hédèik] 名 頭痛

healthy [hélθi] 形 健康な

**hear** [hiər] 動 （～するのを）聞く, 聞こえる　過去形 heard

**heard** [hə:rd] 動 （～するのを）聞いた, 聞こえた　hearの過去形

heart [hɑ:rt] 名 心臓

heat [hi:t] 名 熱　動 熱する

**heavy** [hévi] 形 重い ⇔ light 軽い

held [held] 動 （～を）にぎった, 手に持った　holdの過去形

helicopter [héləkàptər] 名 ヘリコプター

hello [helóu] 間 こんにちは, もしもし（電話）
- *say hello to...* 〜によろしくと伝える

help [help] 動 （〜を）手伝う
- *help mother* [mʌ́ðər] お母さんを手伝う

hen [hen] 名 メンドリ

her [hər] 代 彼女の, 彼女を（に）

here [hiər] 間 さあ 副 ここに

hid [hid] 動 隠れた, （〜を）隠した hideの過去形

hide [haid] 動 隠れる, 隠す 過去形 hid [hid]

hide-and-seek [háid ən sì:k] 名 かくれんぼ

high [hai] 形 （山や建物が）高い ⇔ low 低い

hiking [háikiŋ] 名 ハイキング

him [him] 代 彼を（に）

hippo [hípou] 名 カバ ＝hippopotamus

his [hiz] 代 彼の

hit [hit] 動 （〜を）打つ, たたく 過去形 hit [hit]（同形） 名 打撃

hobby [hábi] 名 趣味（しゅみ）

hold [hould] 動 （〜を）にぎる, 手に持つ 過去形 held [held]

holiday [hálədèi] 名 休日, 祭日

home economics [houm i:kənámiks] 名 家庭科

homework [hóumwə̀:rk] 名 宿題
- *do my homework* （私の）宿題をする

honest [ánist] 形 正直な, 誠意のある

hop [hap] 動 （ぴょんと）はねる, 片足で軽く跳ぶ 過去形 hopped [hapt]

hope [houp] 動 （〜を）のぞむ, （〜を）期待する, ねがう

horizontal bar [hɔ̀(:)rəzántəl ba:r] 名 てつぼう

horse [hɔ:rs] 名 ウマ

hospital [háspitəl] 名 病院

hot [hat] 形 暑い ⇔ cold 寒い
- *hot chocolate* [tʃɔ́:kəlit] ココア
- *hot dog* ホットドッグ

hotel [houtél] 名 ホテル

hour [áuər] 名 時間 *one hour* 1時間

house [haus] 名 家

how [hau] 疑 どのように, どうやって *how to* やり方

how far [háu fá:r] どのくらい（きょり）

how long [háu lɔ́:ŋ] どのくらい（長さ）

how many [háu méni] いくつ（数）

how much [háu mʌ́tʃ] どのくらい（値段・量）

how old [háu óuld] なんさい（年齢）

hug [hʌg] 動 抱きしめる 過去形 hugged [hʌgd]

human being [hjú:mən bí:iŋ] 名 人間

humid [hjú:mid] 形 むしむしした, 湿度の高い

humor [hjú:mər] 名 ユーモア

hung [hʌŋ] 動 （〜を）つるした, ぶらさげた, かけた hangの過去形

hungry [hʌ́ŋgri] 形 おなかがすいた ⇔ full （おなかが）いっぱいの

hurried [hə́:rid] 形 急いだ

hurry [hə́:ri] 動 急ぐ, あわてる 過去形 hurried [hə́:rid]

hurt [hə:rt] 動 傷つく, けがをする, 傷つける 過去形 hurt [hərt]（同形）

husband [hʌ́zbənd] 名 夫

## I i [ai]

I [ai] 代 私は（が）, ぼくは（が）

ice cream [áis kri:m] 名 アイスクリーム

if [if] 接 もしも…なら

ill [il] 形 病気の, （性質・運などが）悪い

important [impɔ́:rtənt] 形 重要な, 大切な

in [in] 前 〜の中に
- *in front of* 〜の正面に

ink [iŋk] 名 インク

insect [ínsekt] 名 こん虫, 虫

interest [íntərist] 名 興味, 関心
- *be interested in...* 興味がある

interesting [íntəristiŋ] 形 おもしろい, 興味深い

international [intərnǽʃənəl] 形 国際的な

introduce [intrədjú:s] 動 紹介する

invent [invént] 動 〜を発明する, 考え出す

invite [inváit] 動 招待する, （〜を）呼ぶ

iron the clothes 服にアイロンをかける

island [áilənd] 名 島

it [it] 代 それは（が）, それを（に）

## J j [dʒei]

jack-o'-lantern [dʒǽkəlæntərn] 名 カボチャのちょうちん

January [dʒǽnjuəri] 名 1月

Japanese [dʒæpaní:z] 名 国語, 日本語 形 日本の

jeans [dʒi:nz] 名 ジーパン, ジーンズ

jet [dʒet] 名 ジェット機

job [dʒab] 名 仕事, 職業

jogging [dʒágiŋ] 名 ジョギング

joke [dʒouk] 名 冗談

juice [dʒu:s] 名 ジュース

July [dʒulái] 名 7月

jump [dʒʌmp] 動 とぶ
- *jump rope* [roup] なわ跳びをする

June [dʒu:n] 名 6月

jungle gym [dʒʌ́ŋgl dʒim] 名 ジャングルジム

## K k [kei]

**kangaroo** [kæ̀ŋgərúː] 名 カンガルー

**keep** [kiːp] 動 (～を)とっておく, (約束を)守る, 続ける
　過去形 kept [kept]

**key** [kiː] 名 かぎ

**kick** [kik] 動 (～を)ける

**kill** [kil] 動 殺す

**kilo** [kí(ː)lou] 名 キロ
　● *kilogram (kg)* [kílougræm] キログラム
　● *kilometer (km)* [kilámətər] キロメートル

**kind** [kaind] 形 親切な, やさしい 名 種類

**kindergarten** [kíndərgàːrtən] 名 幼稚園

**kitchen** [kítʃin] 名 台所

**kite** [kait] 名 凧

**kitten** [kítən] 名 子ネコ

**knee(s)** [niː(z)] 名 ひざ

**knew** [njuː] 動 (～を)知っていた　knowの過去形

**knife** [naif] 名 ナイフ

**knock** [nɑk] 動 ノックする, コツコツたたく

**know** [nou] 動 (～を)知っている　過去形 knew [njuː]

## L l [el]

**lady** [léidi] 名 婦人, 女の人

**ladybug** [léidibÀg] 名 テントウムシ

**laid** [leid] 動 (～を)横たえた, 置いた　layの過去形

**lamp** [læmp] 名 ランプ, 電気スタンド, 照明器具

**language** [læŋgwidʒ] 名 言葉, 言語

**large** [lɑːrdʒ] 形 大きい, 広い

**last** [læst] 形 最後の ⇔ first 最初の

**late** [leit] 形 遅い
　● *be late for...* (～に)遅刻する

**laugh** [læf] 動 (声を出して)笑う

**lawyer** [lɔ́ːjər] 名 弁護士, 法律家

**lay** [lei] 動 横になった, 寝転んだ　lieの過去形

**lay** [lei] 動 (～を)横たえる, 置く　過去形 laid [leid]

**lazy** [léizi] 形 なまけた, なまけものの ● *be lazy* なまける

**leader** [líːdər] 名 リーダー, 指導者

**leaf** [liːf] 名 葉

**learn** [ləːrn] 動 (～を)習う, 学ぶ

**least** [liːst] 形 最も少ない, 最も小さい
　● *at least* 少なくとも

**leave** [liːv] 動 去る, 出発する, (～の状態に)しておく 過去形 left
　● *leave for...* ～へ向かって出発する

**left** [left] 形 左の ⇔ right 右の 動 去った, 出発した,
　(～の状態に)しておいた　leaveの過去形

**leg(s)** [leg(z)] 名 あし

**lemon** [lémən] 名 レモン

**lend** [lend] 動 貸す 過去形 lent [lent]

**lent** [lent] 動 貸した　lendの過去形

**lesson** [lésən] 名 けいこ, 授業

**Let's...** [lets] ～しよう

**letter** [létər] 名 文字, 手紙

**lettuce** [létis] 名 レタス

**library** [láibrəri] 名 図書館

**lie** [lai] 動 横になる 過去形 lay [lei]
　● *lie down* [daun] 寝ころぶ

**lie** [lai] 動 嘘をつく 過去形 lied [laid] 名 嘘

**life** [laif] 名 命, 人生, 生活

**Life Environment Studies** [laif inváiərənmənt stÀdiːz]
　名 生活科

**light** [lait] 形 軽い, 明るい
　名 電灯 ● *light bulb* [bÀlb] 電球

**lighting** [láitniŋ] 名 いなずま, 光

**like** [laik] 動 (～が)好き

**line** [lain] 名 線, 列

**lion** [láiən] 名 ライオン

**listen** [lísən] 動 聞く

**little** [litl] 形 小さい ● *a little* 少しは

**live** [liv] 動 住んでいる

**living room** [líviŋ rùːm] 居間, リビングルーム

**lizard** [lízərd] 名 トカゲ

**long** [lɔːŋ] 形 長い ⇔ short 短い

**look** [luk] 動 見る ● *look at...* ～を見る
　● *look for...* ～をさがす

**loose** [luːz] 形 ゆるい, しまりのない

**lose** [luːz] 動 負ける, なくす 過去形 lost [lɔːst, lɔst]
　● *lose weight* [weit] やせる

**lost** [lɔːst, lɔst] 動 負けた, なくした　loseの過去形

**loudly** [láudli] 副 大声で

**love** [lÀv] 動 (～を)愛している

**lovely** [lÀvli] 形 愛らしい, すてきな

**lunch** [lÀntʃ] 名 昼食, 昼ごはん

## M m [em]

**machine** [məʃíːn] 名 機械
　● *answering machine* [ǽnsəriŋ] 留守番電話

**made** [meid] 動 (～を)作った　makeの過去形

**magazine** [mægəzíːn] 名 雑誌

**mail** [meil] 名 郵便 動 (郵便を)出す

**mailbox** [méilbàks] 名 郵便ポスト

**make** [meik] 動 (～を)作る 過去形 made [meid]

◉ *make the bed* ベッドを整える

**make (a) noise** [nɔiz] 物音を立てる

make friends with... ～と親しくなる

male [meil] 名 男性，（動物の）オス

man [mæn] 名 男の人，人間 　複数形 men [men]

**many** [méni] 形 多い，多数の（数えられる物に使う）

**map** [mæp] 名 地図

marble(s) [maːrbl(z)] 名 ビー玉，おはじき

**March** [maːrtʃ] 名 3月

marry [mǽri] 動 結婚する 　過去形 married [mǽrid]

**math** [mæθ] 名 算数

**May** [mei] 名 5月

**may** [mei] 助 ～してもよい，～かもしれない

maybe [méibi(ː)] 副 たぶん，もしかすると

maze [meiz] 名 迷路

**me** [miː] 代 私に（を），ぼくに（を）

meal [miːl] 名 食事

mean [miːn] 形 意地悪な 動 意味する 過去形 meant [ment]

meant [ment] 動 意味した　mean の過去形

meat [miːt] 名 肉

**mechanical pencil** [məkǽnikəl pènsl] シャープペンシル

**meet** [miːt] 動 （～に）会う 　過去形 met [met]

meeting [míːtiŋ] 名 会，会議

**melon** [mélən] 名 メロン

men [men] 名 男の人，人間　man の複数形

merry [méri] 形 ゆかいな，陽気な

messy [mési] 形 散らかった，乱雑な

**met** [met] 動 （～に）会った　meet の過去形

**mice** [mais] 名 ネズミ　mouse の複数形

midnight [mídnàit] 名 真夜中，夜の12時

**milk** [milk] 名 牛乳

mind [maind] 名 心，精神

**minute** [mínit] 名 （時間の単位）分

Miss [mis] 名 ～さん，～先生（女性で独身の場合）

miss [mis] 動 ～しそこなう，（～が）いなくてさびしい

mistake [mistéik] 名 間違い

◉ *make a mistake* 間違える

mom [mɑm, mɔm] 名 ママ

**Monday** [mʌ́ndei] 名 月曜日

money [mʌ́ni] 名 金

**monkey** [mʌ́ŋki] 名 サル

◉ *monkey bars* [baːrz] うんてい

monster [mɑ́nstər] 名 怪物，モンスター

**month** [mʌnθ] 名 （時間の単位）月

◉ *one month* 1か月

**moon** [muːn] 名 月

more [mɔːr] 形 もっと，もっと多く

**morning** [mɔ́ːrniŋ] 名 朝，午前

◉ *Good morning.* おはよう。

◉ *morning assembly* [əsémbli] 朝礼

mosquito [məskíːtou] 名 蚊（か）

most [moust] 形 いちばん多く

**mother** [mʌ́ðər] 名 お母さん，母

motorbike [móutərbàik] 名 オートバイ

motorcycle [móutərsàikl] 名 オートバイ

**mountain** [máuntin] 名 山

**mouse** [maus] 名 ネズミ 　複数形 mice [mais]

**mouth** [mauθ] 名 口

move [muːv] 動 動く，動かす，引っ越す，感動させる

movie [múːvi] 名 映画

Mr. [místər] 名 ～さん，～氏，～先生（男性の場合）

Mrs. [mísiz] 名 ～さん，～先生，～夫人（女性で結婚している場合）

Ms. [miz] 名 ～さん，～先生（女性の場合）

**much** [mʌtʃ] 形 多い，多量の（数えられない物に使う）

mud [mʌd] 名 泥（どろ）

multiply [mʌ́ltəplài] 動 （掛け算で）～かける

　過去形 multiplied [mʌ́ltəplàid]

◉ *Five times four is twenty.* 5×4＝20

**music** [mjúːzik] 名 音楽

must [mʌst, məst] 助 ～しなければならない，～にちがいない

◉ *mustn't* ～してはいけない

**my** [mai] 代 私の，ぼくの

## N n [en]

name [neim] 名 名前 動 名づける

nature [néitʃər] 名 自然

navy blue [néivi blúː] 名 紺色

near [niər] 形 近い 副 近くに

neck [nek] 名 首

**need** [niːd] 動 （～する）必要がある

nephew [néfjuː] 名 甥（おい）

nest [nest] 名 巣

**never** [névər] 副 決して～でない，絶対～ない

**new** [njuː] 形 新しい ⇔ old 古い

news [njuːz] 名 ニュース

**newspaper** [njúːzpèipər] 名 新聞

next [nekst] 形 次の，となりの

◉ *next week* [wiːk] 来週 ◉ *next month* [mʌnθ] 来月

◉ *next year* [jiər] 来年

**nice** [nais] 形 すてきな

niece [niːs] 名 姪（めい）

night [nait] 名 夜

M
N

ninth [náinθ] 形 9番目の (the ninth)

no [nou] 副 ない, いいえ, (だれも) いない

noise [nɔiz] 名 物音, 雑音

　● *make (a) noise* さわぐ

noisy [nɔ́izi] 形 さわがしい

noodle(s) [nu:dl(z)] 名 めん類

noon [nu:n] 名 正午, 昼の12時

north [nɔ:rθ] 名 北

nose [nouz] 名 鼻

notebook [nóutbùk] 名 ノート

nothing [nʌ́θiŋ] 代 何も～ない

November [nouvémbər] 名 11月

now [nau] 副 いま (では)

number [nʌ́mbər] 名 番号, 数

nurse [nə:rs] 名 看ご師

## O o [ou]

occupation [àkjəpéiʃən] 名 職業, 仕事

ocean [óuʃən] 名 海, 大洋

o'clock [əklák] 副 ～時

October [aktóubər] 名 10月

octopus [áktəpəs] 名 タコ

office clerk [ɔ́(:)fis klə̀:rk] 名 事務員

often [ɔ́(:)fən] 副 しょっちゅう, よく, たびたび

old [ould] 形 年とった

on [ɑn, ən] 前 ～の上に

once [wʌns] 副 一度, 一回　● *at once* さっそく, すぐに

onion [ʌ́njən] 名 たまねぎ

only [óunli] 副 たった, ただ1つだけの

open [óupən] 動 開ける ⇔ close 閉める

opposite [ápəzit] 形 反対の, 向かい側の

orange [ɔ́(:)rindʒ] 名 ミカン, オレンジ色

　● *orange juice* [dʒu:s] オレンジジュース

order [ɔ́:rdər] 動 注文する, 命令する 名 注文, 命令, 順番

other [ʌ́ðər] 形 その他の, 残りの, もう一方の

　● *the other* もうひとつの

our [áuər] 代 私達の, ぼくたちの

out [aut] 副 外へ　● *be out* 留守にする, 外出している

outside [àutsáid] 前 (～の) 外へ　副 外側に

outstanding [àutstǽndiŋ] 形 目立つ (ぬきんでてすごい)

oval [óuvəl] 形 卵形の

oven [ʌ́vən] 名 オーブン

　● レンジは正式には microwave oven (電子レンジ)

over [óuvər] 前 ～の真上に, ～を超えて

　● *over there* [ðéər] 向こうに, あちら

　● *be over* 終わって

overlook [òuvərlúk] 動 見逃す, 見落とす

overseas [òuvərsí:z] 名 海外 形 海外にある, 外国から

oversleep [òuvərslí:p] 動 寝坊する 過去形 overslept

overslept [òuvərslépt] 動 寝坊した　oversleepの過去形

## P p [pi:]

P.E. [p: i:] 名 体育 = Physical Education

page [peidʒ] 名 ページ

paid [peid] 動 (～を) 支払った　payの過去形

paint [peint] 動 (絵の具やペンキで) ぬる

pajamas [pədʒá:məz] 名 パジャマ (必ずsが付く)

pan [pæn] 名 フライパン, (浅い) なべ

pancake(s) [pǽnkèik(s)] 名 パンケーキ

panda [pǽndə] 名 パンダ

pants [pænts] 名 ズボン

paper [péipər] 名 紙

parent [péərənt] 名 親　● *parents* [péərənts] 両親

park [pɑ:rk] 名 公園

　● *amusement park* [əmjú:zmənt] 遊園地

parking lot [lɔt] 駐車場

part [pɑ:rt] 名 部分 動 わかれる

party [pá:rti] 名 パーティー

pass [pæs] 動 渡す, 通り越す, 合格する, ～を超える

past [pæst] 名 過去, 昔　● *in the past* 過去に

paste [peist] 名 のり

pay [pei] 動 (～を) 支払う 過去形 paid [peid]

peace [pi:s] 名 平和

peach [pi:tʃ] 名 モモ

pencil [pénsəl] 名 えんぴつ　● *pencil case* ふでばこ

people [pi:pl] 名 人々

pepper [pépər] 名 コショウ

perfect [pá:rfikt] 形 完璧な, 最高の

　● *perfect score* [skɔ:r] 満点

perhaps [pərhǽps] 副 たぶん

pet [pet] 名 ペット

phone [foun] 名 電話 = telephone [télefoun]

　● *cellular phone* 携帯電話

　● *phone booth* 電話ボックス

photo [fóutou] 名 写真

piano [piǽnou] 名 ピアノ

pick up... [pik əp] ～をひろい上げる

picnic [píknik] 名 ピクニック

picture [píktʃər] 名 絵, 絵画, 写真

piece [pi:s] 名 ひときれ, かけら

pig [pig] 名 ブタ

pillow [pílou] 名 まくら

**pineapple** [páinæpl] 名 パイナップル

**pink** [piŋk] 名 ピンク

**pizza** [píːtsə] 名 ピザ

**place** [pleis] 名 場所

**plan** [plæn] 名 予定, 計画　動 計画する

**planet** [plǽnit] 名 惑星

**plant** [plænt] 名 植物

**plate** [pleit] 名 皿

**play** [plei] 動 遊ぶ
- *play video games* テレビゲームをする

**play** [plei] 動 (チーム戦のスポーツを)する
- *play soccer* [sákər] サッカーをする
- *play catch* [kætʃ] キャッチボールをする

**play** [plei] 動 (楽器を)ひく
- *play the piano* [piǽnou] ピアノをひく

**playground** [pléigràund] 名 運動場
- *play on the playground* 運動場で遊ぶ

**player** [pléiər] 名 選手

**please** [pliːz] 副 どうぞ

**pocket** [pákit] 名 ポケット

**point** [pɔint] 名 得点

**police officer** [pəlíːs ɔ̀fisər] 警察官

**polite** [pəláit] 形 礼儀正しい

**politician** [pálitíʃən] 名 政治家

**pond** [pɑnd] 名 池

**poor** [puər] 名 まずしい ⇔ rich 金持ちの
- *be poor at...* (〜が)下手である

**pop** [pɑp] 名 炭酸飲料

**popular** [pápjulər] 形 人気のある

**postcard** [póustkà:rd] 名 ハガキ, ポストカード

**post office** [póust ɔ(:)fis] 郵便局

**pot** [pɑt] 名 深いなべ(浅いなべは pan)

**potato** [pətéitou] 名 じゃがいも

**practice** [prǽktis] 動 (〜の)練習をする, けいこする

**prepare** [pripéər] 動 用意する, 準備する

**present** [prézənt] 名 プレゼント

**president** [prézidənt] 名 大統領

**pretty** [príti] 形 かわいい

**price** [prais] 名 ねだん

**pride** [praid] 名 誇り

**principal** [prínsəpəl] 名 校長先生

**problem** [prábləm] 名 問題

**program** [próugræm] 名 番組

**promise** [prámis] 動 約束する

**(be) proud of...** [práud əv] (〜を)誇りに思う

**puddle** [pʌdl] 名 水たまり

**pull** [pul] 動 (〜を)引く ⇔ push (〜を)押す

**pumpkin** [pʌ́mpkin] 名 かぼちゃ

**pupa** [pjúːpə] 名 さなぎ

**puppy** [pʌ́pi] 名 子犬

**purple** [pə́:rpl] 名 紫色

**purpose** [pə́:rpəs] 名 目的　◦ *on purpose* わざと

**push** [puʃ] 動 (〜を)押す ⇔ pull (〜を)引く

**put** [put] 動 置く　過去形 put [put](同形)
- *put...on...* 〜に〜を乗せる　◦ *put off* 延ばす
- *put away* [əwéi] 〜をかたづける

**put off** [ɔ:f] 延期する

**put on...** (シャツなどを)着る, (くつなどを)はく
- *put on shoes* [ʃuːz] くつをはく

# Q q [kjuː]

**question** [kwéstʃən] 名 質問

**quickly** [kwíkli] 副 すばやく, すぐに

**quiet** [kwáiət] 形 静かな ⇔ noisy さわがしい
- *be quiet* 静かにする

# R r [ɑːr]

**rabbit** [rǽbit] 名 ウサギ

**racket** [rǽkit] 名 ラケット

**rain** [rein] 名 雨　動 雨がふる

**rainbow** [réinbòu] 名 虹

**raincoat** [réinkòut] 名 レインコート

**rainy** [réini] 形 (天気)雨ふりの

**ran** [ræn] 動 走った　runの過去形

**rat** [ræt] 名 ネズミ(どぶねずみなどの大型のネズミ)

**reach** [ríːtʃ] 動 着く, 到着する

**read** [riːd] 動 (〜を)読む　過去形 read [red] ※発音注意
- *read comics* [kámiks] マンガを読む

**ready** [rédi] 形 用意ができて

**really** [ríːəli, ríəli] 副 本当に

**reason** [ríːzən] 名 理由

**receive** [risíːv] 動 〜を受け取る

**record** [rikɔ́:rd] 動 〜を記録する, 〜を録音(録画)する　名 [ríkɔ:rd] 記録(名詞ではアクセントが異なることに注意)

**rectangle** [réktæ̀ŋgl] 名 長方形

**recycle** [rìːsáikl] 動 リサイクル

**red** [red] 名 赤

**relative** [rélətiv] 名 親戚

**relay** [ríːlei] 名 リレー

**remember** [rimémbər] 動 (〜を)覚えている

**repeat** [ripíːt] 動 繰り返す

**report** [ripɔ́:rt] 名 報告　動 報告する

reservation [rèzərvéiʃən] 名 予約

reserve [rizə́:rv] 動 （〜を）予約する

respect [rispékt] 動 （〜を）尊敬する

rest [rest] 名 休み, 休憩

**restaurant** [réstərənt] 名 レストラン

return [ritə́:rn] 動 戻す, 戻る

rice [rɑis] 名 ごはん　◉ *rice cooker* [kúkər] 炊飯器

**rich** [ritʃ] 形 金持ちの ⇔ poor まずしい

**ride** [rɑid] 動 （自転車や馬に）乗る　過去形 rode [roud]
　　◉ *ride a bike*　自転車に乗る

**right** [rɑit] 形 右の, 正しい ⇔ wrong まちがった

ring [riŋ] 名 指輪

rise [rɑiz] 動 上がる, 昇る　過去形 rose [rouz]

**river** [rívər] 名 川

road [roud] 名 道, 道路

robot [róubət] 名 ロボット

**rocket** [rάkit] 名 ロケット

**rode** [roud] 動 （自転車などに）乗った　ride の過去形

roof [ru:f] 名 屋根

room [ru:m] 名 部屋

root [ru:t] 名 根, （theを前に付けて）根底, 原因

rose [rouz] 動 上がった, 昇った　rise の過去形　名 バラ

round [raund] 形 丸い

row [rou] 名 列

rowboat [róubòut] 名 船, （手こぎの）ボート

rude [ru:d] 形 失礼な

rug [rʌg] 名 ラグ, 小さい敷きもの

rule [ru:l] 名 ルール

**ruler** [rú:lər] 名 じょうぎ

**run** [rʌn] 動 走る　過去形 ran [ræn]

**run away**　逃げる　過去形 ran away

# S s [es]

**sad** [sæd] 形 悲しい

safe [seif] 形 安全な　名 金庫

**said** [sed] 動 言った　say の過去形

**salad** [sǽləd] 名 サラダ

**salt** [sɔ:lt] 名 塩

sand [sænd] 名 砂

**sandwich** [sǽndwitʃ] 名 サンドイッチ

**sang** [sæŋ] 動 歌った　sing の過去形

Santa Claus [sǽntə klɔ̀:z] 名 サンタクロース

**sat** [sæt] 動 すわった　sit の過去形

**Saturday** [sǽtərdei] 名 土曜日

**say** [sei] 動 言う　過去形 said [sed]

**saw** [sɔ:] 動 （〜を）見た, （〜に）会った　see の過去形

scarf [skɑ:rf] 名 マフラー

**scary** [skéəri] 形 こわい

**school** [sku:l] 名 学校

**school bag** [skú:l bæg] 名 通学用かばん

**science** [sáiəns] 名 理科

**scientist** [sáiəntist] 名 科学者

**scissors** [sízərz] 名 はさみ

scold [skould] 動 しかる

score [skɔ:r] 名 成績, 得点

scratch [skrætʃ] 動 ひっかく

sea [si:] 名 海　◉ *sea otter* [άtər] ラッコ

season [sí:zən] 名 季節
　　◉ *the rainy season* [réini] 梅雨（つゆ）

seat [si:t] 名 席

**second** [sékənd] 形 2番目の（the second）名 （時間の単位）秒

secret [sí:krit] 形 秘密の　名 秘密

**see** [si:] 動 （〜を）見る, （〜に）会う　過去形 saw [sɔ:]
　　◉ *see a doctor* [dάktər] 医者にかかる

seem [si:m] 動 らしい, 〜のようだ

**seldom** [séldəm] 副 めったに〜しない, たまに

**seesaw** [sí:sɔ:] 名 シーソー

selfish [sélfiʃ] 形 わがままな

**sell** [sel] 動 （〜を）売る　過去形 sold [sould]

**send** [send] 動 （〜を）送る　過去形 sent [sent]

sentence [séntəns] 名 文章

**sent** [sent] 動 （〜を）送った　send の過去形

**September** [septémbər] 名 9月

serious [síəriəs] 形 真面目な, 本気の

set [set] 動 （〜を）置く, セットする　過去形 set [set]（同形）
　　◉ *set the table*　食卓の準備をする

**seventh** [sévənθ] 形 7番目の（the seventh）

shake [ʃeik] 動 振る　過去形 shook [ʃuk]

share [ʃeər] 動 分ける

**she** [ʃi:] 代 彼女は, 彼女が

**sheep** [ʃi:p] 名 ヒツジ　単複同形 sheep [ʃi:p]

shine [ʃain] 動 輝く　過去形 shone [ʃoun]

**ship** [ʃip] 名 船

shirt [ʃə:rt] 名 シャツ

**shoe(s)** [ʃu:(z)] 名 くつ　◉ *shoe store* [stɔ́:r] 靴屋

shone [ʃoun] 動 輝いた　shine の過去形

shook [ʃuk] 動 振った　shake の過去形

**short** [ʃɔ:rt] 形 短い, （背が）低い

should [ʃəd, ʃud] 助 〜すべき

shoulder [ʃóuldər] 名 肩

**shout** [ʃaut] 動 叫ぶ

shut [ʃʌt] 動 閉める, とじる　過去形 shut [ʃʌt]（同形）

R
S

**sick** [sik] 形 病気の

silent [sáilənt] 形 静かな, だまった

silly [síli] 形 ばかな

simple [simpl] 形 簡単な, わかりやすい, 質素な

**sing** [siŋ] 動 歌う 過去形 sang [sæŋ]

singer [síŋər] 名 歌手

sister [sístər] 名 姉妹

   ● *big sister* 姉   ● *little sister* 妹

**sit** [sit] 動 すわる 過去形 sat [sæt]

**sixth** [siksθ] 形 6番目の (the sixth)

size [saiz] 名 サイズ

**skate** [skeit] 動 スケートをする

skateboarding [skéitbɔ̀ːrdiŋ] 名 スケートボード (競技)

skating [skéitiŋ] 名 スケート (競技)

**ski** [skiː] 動 スキーをする

**skiing** [skíːiŋ] 名 スキー (競技)

**skip** [skip] 動 スキップをする 過去形 skipped [skipt]

**skirt** [skəːrt] 名 スカート

**sky** [skai] 名 空

**sleep** [sliːp] 動 ねむる 過去形 slept [slept]

**sleepy** [slíːpi] 形 ねむい

**slept** [slept] 動 ねむった sleep の過去形

**slide** [slaid] 動 すべる 過去形 slid [slid] 名 すべり台

slipper(s) [slípər(z)] 名 スリッパ (通常 s を付けて slippers)

slow [slou] 形 おそい ⇔ fast 速い

**slowly** [slóuli] 副 ゆっくり, おそく

**small** [smɔːl] 形 小さい ⇔ big 大きい

**smell** [smel] 動 におう, においがする

**smile** [smail] 動 (にっこり) 笑う, ほほえむ

smoke [smouk] 名 煙 動 タバコをすう

**snake** [sneik] 名 ヘビ

**sneaker(s)** [sníːkər(z)] 名 運動ぐつ

**sneeze** [sniːz] 名 くしゃみ 動 くしゃみをする

**snow** [snou] 名 雪

**snowy** [snóui] 形 (天気) 雪のふる

soap [soup] 名 石けん

**soccer** [sákər] 名 サッカー

   ● *soccer player* [pléiər] サッカー選手

**social studies** [sóuʃəl stʌ̀diəz] 社会科

**sock(s)** [sak(s)] 名 くつした

**sofa** [sóufə] 名 ソファ

soft [sɔ(ː)ft] 形 やわらかい ⇔ hard 硬い

   ● *soft drink* 清涼飲料水

**sold** [sould] 動 (〜を) 売った sell の過去形

solve [salv, sɔlv] 動 (〜を) 解決する

some [sʌm, səm] 形 いくつかの

someone [sʌ́mwʌ̀n] 代 だれか

something [sʌ́mθiŋ] 代 何か

sometimes [sʌ́mtàimz] 副 ときどき

son [sʌn] 名 息子

song [sɔ(ː)ŋ] 名 歌

soon [suːn] 副 すぐに, そのうち

sorry [sɔ́ːri] 形 ごめんなさい, 残念な

sound [saund] 名 音 動 鳴る

soup [suːp] 名 スープ

south [sauθ] 名 南

souvenir [sùːvəníər] 名 みやげ

space [speis] 名 宇宙

**spaghetti** [spəgéti] 名 スパゲティ

**speak** [spiːk] 動 (〜を) 話す 過去形 spoke [spouk]

   ● *speak English* 英語を話す

special [spéʃəl] 形 とくべつな

spend [spend] 動 費やす, 使う 過去形 spent [spent]

spent [spent] 動 費やした, 使った spend の過去形

**spider** [spáidər] 名 クモ

**spinach** [spínitʃ] 名 ホウレンソウ

**spoke** [spouk] 動 (〜を) 話した speak の過去形

**spoon** [spuːn] 名 スプーン

**sport** [spɔːrt] 名 スポーツ

**spring** [spriŋ] 名 春

square [skweər] 名 正方形, 広場

**stand** [stænd] 動 立つ 過去形 stood [stud]

staple [steipl] 動 ホッチキスでとめる

**stapler** [stéiplər] 名 ホッチキス

**star** [staːr] 名 星

**start** [staːrt] 動 出発する, 始まる, 始める

**stay** [stei] 動 滞在する, とどまる

   ● *stay at...* (〜に) 滞在する

   ● *stay at home* 留守番をする

**stay up late** 夜ふかしする

steak [steik] 名 ステーキ

steal [stiːl] 動 盗む 過去形 stole [stoul]

steam [stiːm] 動 むす, ふかす

stew [stjuː] 動 とろ火で煮る

stick [stik] 名 棒

stingy [stíndʒi] 形 けちな

stole [stoul] 動 盗んだ steal の過去形

stomachache [stʌ́məkèik] 名 腹痛

**stood** [stud] 動 立った stand の過去形

**stop** [stap] 動 止まる, (〜を) やめる 過去形 stopped [stapt]

**stove** [stouv] 名 こんろ, ガスレンジ

strange [streindʒ] 形 変な

**strawberry** [strɔ́ːbèri] 名 イチゴ

street [striːt] 名 通り, 街路

stretch [stretʃ] 動 伸ばす

**strict** [strict] 形 きびしい

**strong** [strɔ(:)ŋ] 形 強い ⇔ weak [wi:k] 弱い

student [stjú:dənt] 名 学生, 生徒

**study** [stʌ́di] 動 (〜を)勉強する 過去形 studied [stʌ́did]
- ○ *study abroad* 留学する

succeed [səksí:d] 動 成功する

suddenly [sʌ́dnli] 副 突然, 急に

**sugar** [ʃúɡər] 名 さとう

**subway** [sʌ́bwèi] 名 地下鉄
- ○ イギリスでは *underground* [ʌ́ndərɡràund] と言う

**summer** [sʌ́mər] 名 夏

sumo wrestler [réslər] 相撲取り, 力士

**sun** [sʌn] 名 太陽 (the sun)

**Sunday** [sʌ́ndei] 名 日曜日

**sunny** [sʌ́ni] 形 (天気)日が照っている, 天気のよい

**supermarket** [sú:pərmà:rkit] 名 スーパーマーケット

supper [sʌ́pər] 名 夕食

**sure** [ʃuər] 形 確信している 副 もちろん, 確かに, きっと
- ○ *make sure* 確かめる

surprise [sərpráiz] 動 おどろかせる
- ○ *be surprised at...* 〜におどろく, びっくりする

swam [swʌm] 動 泳いだ swimの過去形

**sweater** [swétər] 名 セーター

**swim** [swim] 動 泳ぐ 過去形 swam [swæm]

**swimming** [swímiŋ] 名 水泳
- ○ *swimming pool* [pu:l] プール

**swing** [swiŋ] 名 ブランコ 動 振る, ゆれる
過去形 swung [swʌŋ]

swung [swʌŋ] 動 振った, ゆれた swingの過去形

# T t [ti:]

**table** [teibl] 名 テーブル, 食卓
- ○ *set the table* 食卓の準備をする
- ○ *table tennis* 卓球 =Ping-Pong

**take** [teik] 動 (〜を)取る, 持って行く, (時間が)かかる
過去形 took [tuk]

**take a bath** ふろに入る

**take a nap** 昼寝をする

**take a walk** 散歩する

**take care of...** 〜の世話をする

take off... (〜を)脱ぐ ○ *take off shoes* くつを脱ぐ

take out... (〜を)出す ○ *take out a book* 本を取り出す

**talk** [tɔ:k] 動 しゃべる, 話す

**tall** [tɔ:l] 形 (人や木が)高い ⇔ short 低い

taste [teist] 動 味がする 名 味

**taught** [tɔ:t] 動 (〜を)教えた teachの過去形

**taxi driver** [tæksi dràivər] タクシー運転手

**tea** [ti:] 名 茶, 紅茶

**teach** [ti:tʃ] 動 (〜を)教える 過去形 taught [tɔ:t]

**teacher** [tí:tʃər] 名 教師, 先生

tear [teər] 動 破れる, 裂ける 過去形 tore [tɔ:r, tɔə]
- ○ *tear up* 破る, 引き裂く

tear [tiər] 名 涙 ※発音注意

**teeth** [ti:θ] 名 歯 toothの複数形

**telephone** [téləfòun] 名 電話 =phone [foun]

telescope [téləskòup] 名 望遠鏡

**television** [téləvìʒən] 名 テレビ (一般的にはT.V.)

**tell** [tel] 動 (〜を)話す, (〜を)伝える 過去形 told [tould]

**tennis** [ténis] 名 テニス

**tenth** [tenθ] 形 10番目の (the tenth)

**textbook** [tékstbùk] 名 教科書, テキスト

thank [θæŋk] 動 感謝する

that [ðæt, ðət] 代 あれ, あちら 複数形 those 形 あの

their [ðeər, ðər] 代 彼らの, 彼女達の

them [ðem, ðəm] 代 彼らを (に), 彼女達を (に)

then [ðen] 副 その時, それから, それでは

there [ðeər, ðər] 副 〜がある, そこに

these [ði:z] 代 これら thisの複数形

**they** [ðei] 代 彼らは (が), 彼女達は (が)

thick [θik] 形 厚い ⇔ thin [θin] 薄い

thief [θi:f] 名 どろぼう

thin [θin] 形 細い ⇔ thick [θik] 厚い

thing [θiŋ] 名 物, こと

**think** [θiŋk] 動 (〜と)思う, (〜であると)考える
過去形 thought [θɔ:t]

**third** [θə:rd] 形 3番目の (the third)

**thirsty** [θə́:rsti] 形 のどがかわいた

this [ðis] 代 これ, こちら 複数形 these [ði:z] 形 この

those [ðouz] 代 あれら thatの複数形

**thought** [θɔ:t] 動 (〜と)思った, (〜であると)考えた
thinkの過去形

**threw** [θru:] 動 (〜を)投げた throwの過去形

throat [θrout] 名 のど

**throw** [θrou] 動 (〜を)投げる 過去形 threw [θru:]

thumb [θʌm] 名 親指

thunder [θʌ̀ndər] 名 雷

**Thursday** [θə́:rzdei] 名 木曜日

ticket [tíkit] 名 切符, チケット

tie [tai] 名 ネクタイ 動 結ぶ

**tiger** [táigər] 名 トラ

tight [tait] 形 きつい, しっかりと

**time** [taim] 名 時間, 時刻

**tired** [táiərd] 形 疲れた

**tissue** [tíʃuː] 名 ティッシュペーパー

**toast** [toust] 名 トースト, 乾杯(かんぱい) 動 こんがりと焼く

**today** [tədéi] 名 今日

**toe** [tou] 名 足の指

**together** [təgéðər] 副 一緒に

**told** [tould] 動 (～を)話した, (～を)伝えた　tell の過去形

**tomato** [təméitou] 名 トマト

**tomorrow** [təmárou] 名 明日

**tonight** [tənáit] 名 今晩

**too** [tuː] 副 ～もまた, あまりに～

**took** [tuk] 動 (～を)取った, 持って行った, (時間が)かかった　take の過去形

**tooth** [tuːθ] 名 歯　複数形 teeth [tiːθ]

**toothbrush** [túːθbrʌʃ] 名 歯ブラシ

**toothpaste** [túːθpèist] 名 歯みがき粉

**tore** [tɔːr, tɔə] 動 破れた, 裂けた　tear の過去形

**touch** [tʌtʃ] 動 さわる, 触れる 名 感触

**towel** [táuəl] 名 タオル

**town** [taun] 名 町

**toy** [tɔi] 名 おもちゃ

**track** [træk] 名 陸上競技

**traffic light** [træfik làit] 名 信号

**train** [trein] 名 電車　● *train station* [stéiʃən] 電車の駅

**travel** [trævəl] 動 旅行する 名 旅 ＝trip

**tray** [trei] 名 トレー, 盆

**treasure** [tréʒər] 名 宝物

**tree** [triː] 名 木

**triangle** [tráiæŋgl] 名 三角形, (楽器の)トライアングル

**tried** [traid] 動 試した, ～しようとした　try の過去形

**truck** [trʌk] 名 トラック

**true** [truː] 形 本当の

**try** [trai] 動 試す, ～しようとする　過去形 tried [traid]

**Tuesday** [tjúːzdei] 名 火曜日

**turn** [təːrn] 動 回転する, 回る 名 番(順番)
    ● *turn on / off the light*　明かりをつける/消す

**twelfth** [twelfθ] 形 12番目の (the twelfth)

**twice** [twais] 副 2度, 2倍

**twins** [twinz] 名 ふたご

## U u [juː]

**ugly** [Ágli] 形 みにくい

**umbrella** [ʌmbrélə] 名 かさ

**uncle** [Áŋkl] 名 おじ

**under** [Ándər] 前 ～の下に

**underpants** [Ándərpænts] 名 下着のパンツ

**understand** [ʌndərstænd] 動 (～を)理解する, わかる
  過去形 understood [ʌndərstúd]

**understood** [ʌndərstúd] 動 (～を)理解した, わかった
  understand の過去形

**universe** [júːnivəːrs] 名 宇宙 (the universe)

**university** [jùːnivəːrsəti] 名 大学

**upside down** [ʌpsaid dáun] さかさまの

**upstairs** [Ápstéərz] 副 2階に(で)
    ● *Go upstairs.*　2階に行きなさい。

**us** [ʌs, əs] 代 私達に(を), ぼくたちに(を)

**use** [juːz] 動 (～を)使う

**useful** [júːsfəl] 形 役立つ

**usually** [júːʒuəli] 副 ふつうは, いつもは

## V v [viː]

**vacation** [veikéiʃən] 名 休暇, 休み

**vacuum cleaner** [vækjuəm klíːnər] そうじ機
    ● *vacuum the room*　部屋にそうじ機をかける

**vegetable** [védʒitəbl] 名 野菜

**very** [véri] 副 とても, 非常に

**video game** [vídiòu geim] テレビゲーム

**village** [vílidʒ] 名 村

**violin** [vàiəlín] 名 バイオリン

**visit** [vízit] 動 訪れる, 訪問する

**voice** [vɔis] 名 声

**volcano** [vɑlkéinou] 名 火山

**volleyball** [válibɔ̀ːl] 名 バレーボール

## W w [dʌ́bljuː]

**wait** [weit] 動 待つ　● *wait for...*　～を待つ

**wake up** 目をさます

**walk** [wɔːk] 動 歩く

**wall** [wɔːl] 名 かべ

**wallet** [wálit] 名 財布(札入れ) (がま口財布は purse [pəːrs])

**want** [wɑnt] 動 (～が)ほしい

**want to...** ～したい

**war** [wɔːr] 名 戦争

**warm** [wɔːrm] 形 あたたかい

**wash** [wɑʃ] 動 (～を)洗う
    ● *wash the clothes*　洗濯をする
    ● *wash the dishes*　皿を洗う

**watch** [wɑtʃ] 動 見る, 注意して見る 名 腕時計
    ● *watch TV* テレビを見る
    ● *watch the house*　留守番をする

**water** [wɔ́ːtər] 名 水　● *hot water* 湯

T
U
V
W

**watermelon** [wɔ́:tərmèlən] 名 スイカ

**wave** [weiv] 動 手をふる 名 波

**way** [wei] 名 方法, やり方, みち ● *on the way* 途中で

**we** [wi:, wi] 代 私達は(が), ぼくたちは(が)

**weak** [wi:k] 形 弱い ⇔ strong 強い

**wear** [weər] 動 (服を)着ている, 身に付けている
　　過去形 wore [wɔ:r]

**weather** [wéðər] 名 天気

**Wednesday** [wénzdei] 名 水曜日

**week** [wi:k] 名 週, 週間 ● *one week* 1週間

**weekend** [wí:kènd] 名 週末
　　● *on this weekend* この週末に

**weigh** [wei] 動 重さを計る, 重さが～ある

**welcome** [wélkəm] 間 ようこそ

**well** [wel] 副 うまく, 上手に

**went** [went] 動 行った　goの過去形

**west** [west] 名 西

**wet** [wet] 形 ぬれた 動 ぬらす 過去形 wet [wet](同形)

**whale** [hweil] 名 クジラ

**what** [hwat] 疑 何? ● *what time* 何時?

**wheelchair** [hwí:ltʃèər] 名 車いす

**when** [hwen] 疑 いつ?

**where** [hweər] 疑 どこ?

**which** [hwitʃ] 疑 どちら?, どれ?

**whistle** [hwisl] 動 吹く, 口笛を吹く

**white** [hwait] 名 白

**whiteboard** [hwáitbɔ:rd] 名 ホワイトボード

**who** [hu:] 疑 だれ?

**whose** [hu:z] 疑 だれの?

**why** [hwai] 疑 なぜ?

**wide** [waid] 形 (幅が)広い ● *large* (面積が)広い

**wife** [waif] 名 妻

**Will you...?** ～してくれませんか? ～しますか?

**win** [win] 動 勝つ 過去形 won [wʌn]

**wind** [wind] 名 風

**window** [wíndou] 名 窓

**windy** [wíndi] 形 (天気)風の強い

**wine** [wain] 名 ワイン

**wing** [wiŋ] 名 つばさ, 羽

**winter** [wíntər] 名 冬

**wipe** [waip] 動 ふく, ぬぐう

**wish** [wiʃ] 動 (～を)願う, (～であることを)祈る

**witch** [witʃ] 名 魔女

**with** [wið] 前 ～といっしょに

**without** [wiðáut] 前 ～なしで

**woman** [wúmən] 名 女の人

**won** [wʌn] 動 勝った　winの過去形

**wood** [wud] 名 木材

**woods** [wudz] 名 森

**word** [wə:rd] 名 単語

**wore** [wɔ:r] 動 (服を)着ていた, 身に付けていた　wearの過去形

**work** [wə:rk] 動 勉強する, 働く 名 仕事

**world** [wə:rld] 名 世界

**worm** [wə:rm] 名 虫(ミミズなど細長い虫)

**worry** [wə́:ri, wʌ́ri] 動 心配する 過去形 worried [wə́:rid, wʌ́rid]
　　● *worry about* ～のことを心配する

**worse** [wə:rs] 形 もっと悪い

**Would you...?** ～していただけますか?

**write** [rait] 動 (～を)書く 過去形 wrote [rout]

**wrong** [rɔ(:)ŋ] 形 まちがった ⇔ right 正しい

**wrote** [rout] 動 (～を)書いた　writeの過去形

# Y y [wai]

**yacht** [jɑt] 名 ヨット

**yard** [jɑ:rd] 名 庭

**year** [jiər] 名 年 ● *one year* 1年

**yellow** [jélou] 名 黄色

**yesterday** [jéstərdei] 名 昨日

**yet** [jet] 副 まだ～ない(否定文で用いて)

**you** [ju:] 代 あなた(達)は(が), あなた(達)を(に)

**young** [jʌŋ] 形 若い ⇔ old 年とった

**your** [juər, jər] 代 あなた(達)の

# Z z [zi:]

**zebra** [zí:brə] 名 シマウマ

**zero** [zíərou] 名 ゼロ

**zoo** [zu:] 名 動物園

## Numbers

| | | |
|---|---|---|
| 1 **one** [wʌn] | 20 | **twenty** [twénti] |
| 2 **two** [tu:] | 30 | **thirty** [θə́:rti] |
| 3 **three** [θri:] | 40 | **forty** [fɔ́:rti] |
| 4 **four** [fɔ:r] | 50 | **fifty** [fífti] |
| 5 **five** [faiv] | 60 | **sixty** [síksti] |
| 6 **six** [siks] | 70 | **seventy** [sévənti] |
| 7 **seven** [sevn] | 80 | **eighty** [éiti] |
| 8 **eight** [eit] | 90 | **ninety** [náinti] |
| 9 **nine** [nain] | 100 | **one hundred** [wʌn hándred] |
| 10 **ten** [ten] | 1,000 | **one thousand** [wʌn θáuzənd] |
| 11 **eleven** [ilévn] | 10,000 (1万) | **ten thousand** [ten θáuzənd] |
| 12 **twelve** [twelv] | 100,000 (10万) | **one hundred thousand** [wʌn hándred θáuzənd] |
| 13 **thirteen** [θə:rtí:n] | 1,000,000 (100万) | **one million** [wʌn míljən] |
| 14 **fourteen** [fɔ:rtí:n] | 10,000,000 (1000万) | **ten million** [ten míljən] |
| 15 **fifteen** [fiftí:n] | 100,000,000 (1億) | **one hundred million** [wʌn hándred míljən] |
| 16 **sixteen** [sikstí:n] | 1,000,000,000 (10億) | **one billion** [wʌn bíljən] |
| 17 **seventeen** [sevəntí:n] | 10,000,000,000 (100億) | **ten billion** [ten bíljən] |
| 18 **eighteen** [eití:n] | | |
| 19 **nineteen** [naintí:n] | | |

## Ordinal Numbers

| | | |
|---|---|---|
| 1番目の | **first** [fə:rst] | |
| 2番目の | **second** [sékənd] | |
| 3番目の | **third** [θə:rd] | |
| 4番目の | **fourth** [fɔ:rθ] | |
| 5番目の | **fifth** [fifθ] | |
| 6番目の | **sixth** [siksθ] | |
| 7番目の | **seventh** [sévənθ] | |
| 8番目の | **eighth** [eiθ] | |
| 9番目の | **ninth** [nainθ] | |
| 10番目の | **tenth** [tenθ] | |
| 11番目の | **eleventh** [ilévənθ] | |
| 12番目の | **twelfth** [twelfθ] | |

## Countries (Capitals)

※（ ）内は首都名

| | | |
|---|---|---|
| アメリカ合衆国（ワシントンD.C.） | **United States of America** [ju:náitid stéits əv əmérikə] | (Washington, D.C.) |
| アルゼンチン（ブエノスアイレス） | **Argentina** [à:rdʒəntí:nə] | (Buenos Aires) |
| イギリス（ロンドン） | **United Kingdom** [ju:náitid kíŋdəm] | (London) |
| イタリア（ローマ） | **Italy** [ítəli] | (Rome) |
| イラク（バグダッド） | **Iraq** [iræk, irá:k] | (Baghdad) |
| イラン（テヘラン） | **Iran** [iræn, irá:n] | (Teheran) |
| インド（ニューデリー） | **India** [índiə] | (New Delhi) |
| インドネシア（ジャカルタ） | **Indonesia** [ìndəní:ʒə, -zjə] | (Jakarta) |
| エジプト（アディスアベバ） | **Egypt** [í:dʒipt] | (Addis Ababa) |
| オーストラリア（キャンベラ） | **Australia** [ɔ(:)stéiljə] | (Canberra) |
| オランダ（アムステルダム） | **Netherlands** [néðərləndz] | (Amsterdam) |
| カナダ（オタワ） | **Canada** [kǽnədə] | (Ottawa) |
| 韓国（ソウル） | **South Korea** [sauθ kərí(:)ə] | (Seoul) |
| 北朝鮮（平壌） | **North Korea** [nɔ:rθ kərí(:)ə] | (Pyongyang) |
| ケニア（ナイロビ） | **Kenya** [kí:njə] | (Nairobi) |
| サウジアラビア（リヤド） | **Saudi Arabia** [sáudi əréibiə] | (Riyadh) |
| スウェーデン（ストックホルム） | **Sweden** [swi:dən] | (Stockholm) |
| スペイン（マドリッド） | **Spain** [spein] | (Madrid) |
| タイ（バンコク） | **Thailand** [táilænd] | (Bangkok) |
| 台湾（台北） | **Taiwan** [táiwá:n] | (Taipei) |
| 中国（北京） | **China** [tʃáinə] | (Beijing) |
| ドイツ（ベルリン） | **Germany** [dʒə́:rməni] | (Berlin) |
| 日本（東京） | **Japan** [dʒəpǽn] | (Tokyo) |
| ニュージーランド（ウェリントン） | **New Zealand** [nju: zí:lənd] | (Wellington) |
| ノルウェー（オスロ） | **Norway** [nɔ́:rwei] | (Oslo) |
| フィリピン（マニラ） | **Philippine** [fíləpì:n] | (Manila) |
| ブラジル（ブラジリア） | **Brazil** [brəzíl] | (Brasilia) |
| フランス（パリ） | **France** [fræns] | (Paris) |
| ベトナム（ハノイ） | **Vietnam** [víetná:m, -nǽm] | (Hanoi) |
| マレーシア（クアラルンプール） | **Malaysia** [məléiʒiə] | (Kuala Lumpur) |
| メキシコ（メキシコシティー） | **Mexico** [méksəkòu] | (Mexico City) |
| ロシア（モスクワ） | **Russia** [rʌ́sə] | (Moscow) |